Advance praise for *ACT in Steps*

"This manual targets a central challenge of ACT—how to move from learning about the therapy to actually doing it—and hits its mark. It is accessible and concise, offering a session-by-session guide through the therapy from beginning to end, including initial evaluation, ongoing assessment, and between-session homework. The authors provide just the right balance of explanation and practical how-to's needed to set ACT novices on a solid path to competency. In short, it is a perfect answer to, "But, how do I actually do the therapy?" For anyone interested in learning to do ACT—here is your guide."

—**Darrah Westrup**, PhD, author of *Advanced ACT:*
An Experienced Practitioner's Guide to Optimizing
Delivery, co-author of *ACT for the Treatment of Post-Traumatic*
Stress Disorder & Trauma-related problems, *The Mindful Couple*,
and Learning ACT for Group Treatment

"Wow! What a useful and clear guide to starting out in ACT! I wish I'd had this book when I was an ACT newbie—would have saved me so much anxiety, confusion, and self-doubt. (And it also would have saved my clients from so many of the common beginners' mistakes I repeatedly made!) Full of wisdom and packed with practical strategies, I can highly recommend this book for any therapist or counselor who's early on in their ACT journey."

—**Russ Harris**, author of *The Happiness Trap*

"The authors are right: I have always said that the best way to begin actually *doing* ACT (after experiential contact with it and exposure to its principles) is to follow a step-by-step manual with several cases. That ensures you will practice all aspects of the approach and it distills the learning process down to smaller bits that are easier to handle. There are other beginning ACT manuals out there but this may now be my favorite. Thorough and yet simple, this well-written and wise volume gently pushes you forward to learn ACT, one step at a time. Highly recommended."

—**Steven C. Hayes**, Foundation Professor of Psychology,
University of Nevada, Reno, Originator and co-developer
of Acceptance and Commitment Therapy

ACT in Steps

A Transdiagnostic Manual for Learning
Acceptance and Commitment Therapy

MICHAEL P. TWOHIG, MICHAEL E. LEVIN,

AND CLARISSA W. ONG

OXFORD
UNIVERSITY PRESS

Oxford University Press is a department of the University of Oxford. It furthers
the University's objective of excellence in research, scholarship, and education
by publishing worldwide. Oxford is a registered trade mark of Oxford University
Press in the UK and certain other countries.

Published in the United States of America by Oxford University Press
198 Madison Avenue, New York, NY 10016, United States of America.

© Oxford University Press 2021

Library of Congress Cataloging-in-Publication Data
Names: Twohig, Michael P., author. | Levin, Michael E., author. | Ong, Clarissa W., author.
Title: ACT in steps : a transdiagnostic manual for learning acceptance and
commitment therapy / Michael P. Twohig, Michael E. Levin, Clarissa W. Ong.
Other titles: Acceptance and commitment therapy in steps
Description: New York : Oxford University Press, [2021] |
Includes bibliographical references and index.
Identifiers: LCCN 2020010447 (print) | LCCN 2020010448 (ebook) |
ISBN 9780190629922 (paperback) | ISBN 9780190668990 (epub) |
ISBN 9780190629946
Subjects: LCSH: Acceptance and commitment therapy. | Psychotherapy.
Classification: LCC RC489.A32 T96 2021 (print) | LCC RC489.A32 (ebook) |
DDC 616.89/1425—dc23
LC record available at https://lccn.loc.gov/2020010447
LC ebook record available at https://lccn.loc.gov/2020010448

9 8 7 6 5 4 3 2 1
Printed by Marquis, Canada

CONTENTS

The idea for this book came to me at the end of a workshop I (M.P.T.) was delivering in Augusta, Georgia, to a group of Army psychologists and other mental health professionals who work at the Veterans Administration. This was a training event where someone higher up invited me and the audience was informed that they were required to attend the training. These are always interesting situations because the curiosity in the topic varies among the audience members. Some are really pleased that training on ACT is being offered, whereas others have never heard of ACT before or are not interested in it. In general, these audience members in Augusta were skeptically open; they were hopeful that the training would be useful to them and the people they serve, but they were not going to simply buy into whatever I was saying.

The two days went quite well. We talked about working with posttraumatic stress disorder (PTSD), wounded warriors, chronic pain, depression, substance abuse, and many other topics. I taught the audience about philosophy of science, the theory of ACT, its basic and applied research, and when to use ACT and when not to. Most of our time was spent on how to implement ACT. As anyone who has attended a training—even a multi-day one—knows, you are not going to be good at that therapy (or whatever the training is on) after one event. I knew this from my own postgraduate training where I experienced the same thing, but something one of the audience members said really stuck with me. I remember this postdoctoral intern vividly. I still know where he was sitting, what he looked like, and the type of clients with whom he worked. His words stuck with me because it was in that moment I knew there was a gap in our ACT training. I had just completed a two-day training on ACT. We did lots of role-plays. I demonstrated everything. At the end of all this he asked me, "How do I go and do this with my clients?"

I felt disheartened. I worked hard for two days to teach these professionals how to do ACT. They spent money and time on the workshop, yet the intern did not know where to start, much less how to conduct multiple sessions of ACT. The attendees knew many important things about ACT. They could identify the six important treatment processes in clients. They even knew ways to build the target processes. Still, the intern did not know what to say in session one and how to logically build on that.

Even as the trainer of that workshop and many others, I have to agree with him. I have never been able to walk out of a training and do the thing that was taught. I usually learned that the topic was interesting, I liked it, and I was interested in it, but not how to go and do it. This training gap is exacerbated by the fact that the instructor leaves after the training. This intern was left on his own. He stayed in Georgia while I flew back to Utah. I felt frustrated because I get a question like this at almost every training I give. Maybe other trainers are more talented than me and their attendees can implement the therapy after their workshops. However, if this is not the case, then there are many people who have learned enough about ACT to have an interest in it but lack the resources to actually implement it. I tell attendees the same thing:

> ACT is a therapeutic model that orients to a set of key processes to work on with clients, rather than a protocol with prescribed techniques, so there is no manual. There are six processes of change that you should assess for in your client. Then, you assess the degree to which those processes are affecting the treatment target. You should use any variety of ACT techniques to influence the pertinent processes of change. As those processes shift in the desired direction, you should see improvements in the treatment target. There are books that describe ACT for different clinical presentations which should offer some guidance. The issue is: with the exception of a few books, ACT is explained by each process, rather than by session. This is great in every way except for learning how to do it. There are a couple self-help books that explain it session-by-session. Maybe reading those will help you understand what ACT looks like in real life. There are also videos, but they are really expensive. You can find a few online. Also, join ACBS (Association for Contextual Behavioral Science) because there is lots of good material there and their membership fee is quite low.

This is an odd thing to say to someone after they spend two days getting trained! I am basically saying, "If you want to start doing ACT, you are going to need to start studying." Everything is available, but you are going to need to make sense of it. Mike Levin and I went to graduate school at the University of Nevada, under the supervision of Steven Hayes, who is primarily associated with the development of ACT. Guess how we learned to do ACT? We followed a manual! I followed a manual on ACT for about two years before I slowly started to understand what was going on in ACT. My actions were shaped by the client and my supervisors. I got better at seeing the six processes of change and thinking about what needed to be targeted next. I started saying things that were not in the manual but from books, videos, or what I learned from my colleagues. The flow of sessions got smoother. I started doing ACT. Now, I teach a graduate course on

ACT and supervise a practicum on ACT. Newer therapists follow manuals or self-help books as they get going.

All this is a long-winded way of saying: We think it is just fine—even wise—to start doing ACT by following a manual. Somehow your interest was piqued. Maybe you attended a training on ACT, you read an article or two, or this book was assigned to you in a graduate course. Nonetheless, you are going to start using this approach with your clients. We hope that this book will be a useful guide through your first five or so clients. You will learn how ACT works, when the key processes of change are present, how to move those processes, and when the session feels meaningful, among other things. You will start to see what you do and do not know, and you can find ways to improve those skills. This book is your stabilizer—your training wheels—to get you started. This book is hopefully more useful than a manual because it is written for a novice learning how to do ACT. We hope it is also more useful than following a self-help book because it is written for a therapist, not a client. We hope this book is what you need for the beginning before you move on to more advanced material. Good luck!

What Is Acceptance and Commitment Therapy (ACT)?

We will give a broad overview of ACT in this first chapter. This will include how ACT fits into the broader empirically supported therapy and evidence-based practice literature, such as how ACT overlaps with other treatments and defining qualities that distinguish it. We will also give you a primer on the basics of ACT theory, providing you with an overall sense of the model. By the end of the chapter, we want you to have a sense of what ACT is and of the basic concepts and terms used throughout this book.

IS THIS A REASONABLE CHOICE FOR THERAPY?

There are many factors that go into choosing a therapy for a given client and as part of your broader collection of approaches you will use. You might consider what the evidence base is for the specific presenting concern, whether it fits well with your existing training and approach to working with clients, and whether it applies well to the clients you serve. Part of our enthusiasm for ACT is due to how well it can fit for so many therapists as (1) an empirically supported treatment that (2) applies to a wide range of clients with various struggles and (3) is flexible in how it fits a variety of therapeutic approaches and backgrounds. There is also a style to ACT that fits quite well for certain clients. Understanding how to do ACT well and when to use it should help you professionally.

ACT is an empirically supported treatment (EST)

Over the past two decades, research on ACT has skyrocketed, with over 300 published randomized control trials (RCTs) to date demonstrating the efficacy of ACT for a range of problems including depression, anxiety disorders, obsessive-compulsive and related disorders, psychosis, addictions, eating disorders, stigma, stress and burnout, chronic pain, weight loss, and coping with or managing medical conditions (Association for Contextual Behavioral Science [ACBS], 2019). Meta-analyses of ACT show that it produces large effect sizes when compared to waitlists, and small to medium effect sizes relative to active control conditions such as treatment-as-usual (A-Tjak et al., 2015; Bluett, Homan, Morrison, Levin, & Twohig, 2014; Hughes, Clark, Colclough, Dale, & McMillan, 2017; Lee, An, Levin, & Twohig, 2015). Compared to other empirically supported cognitive-behavioral therapies (CBTs), ACT generally performs equivalently (Bluett et al., 2014), with a slight, nonsignificant trend suggesting ACT may have stronger effects than other CBTs and established treatments in some cases (A-Tjak et al., 2015; Lee et al., 2015). As of 2019, the official list of ESTs from Division 12 of the American Psychological Association indicated that ACT is evidence-based for anxiety disorders, depression, chronic pain, psychosis, and obsessive-compulsive disorder (although this list is slow and conservative to update). Thus, the evidence base of ACT is positive, continues to grow exponentially, and is consistent with evidence-based practice.

Broad applicability to clients

As you will find throughout this book, ACT is defined functionally in terms of a set of mindfulness, acceptance, and values-based processes applied to target maladaptive ways in which clients "get stuck" in their lives. The ways clients get stuck can be found across a wide range of presentations and settings, and the ways we help clients get unstuck in ACT similarly work well across a breadth of areas. Just like a client might get stuck in an avoidance cycle with their depression, they can get stuck with cravings, anxiety, pain, body image concerns, adhering to a medication, and so on. The evidence bears this out too showing these maladaptive processes (e.g., emotional avoidance, inaction, rumination) targeted by ACT predict a wide range of problems, and using ACT to target these processes leads to improvements in a variety of clinical presentations (A-Tjak et al., 2015; Bluett et al., 2014; Hayes, Levin, Plumb-Vilardaga, Villatte, & Pistorello, 2013; Twohig & Levin, 2017). In later chapters, we will explore how to assess and conceptualize cases based on the ACT model, but suffice it to say, ACT can be applied to a range of clients and is thus likely to be useful in whatever setting you work in.

ACT is flexible in applying to a wide range of practitioners

As a functional approach, ACT not only applies to a wide range of clients but also fits a wide range of practitioners. There are *many* ways to do ACT, such that it can align with different personal styles, therapeutic strategies, settings, and clients. What matters is function—helping clients be more mindful and accepting of their experiences while doing what is meaningful and effective in the moment. This can look deeply experiential and relational, psychoeducational and didactic, and anywhere in between depending on various factors. Therapists regularly tell us how they use their existing skills and strategies from other treatments to do ACT (e.g., psychodynamic, humanistic, cognitive-behavioral, systems, multicultural) or that they recognize techniques used in ACT protocols from other approaches. What matters is that your therapist behaviors serve to move ACT targets (which we often refer to as "function over form"). This flexibility, at times, can feel overwhelming given all the choices available, but the flexibility also means it is a lot more likely that ACT can be fitted to the type of therapy you practice and clients with whom you work. If you are in a primary care setting, rest assured, ACT can be adapted to that type of brief, focused format. If you are in community mental health, ACT can be adapted to the unique needs of clients from various backgrounds. As a reflection of this flexibility, ACT is increasingly being adopted by professions across and outside of healthcare, including behavior analysis, social work, nursing, education, criminal justice, athletics, workplaces, and so on.

This book aims to give an introduction to ACT as an evidence-based, flexible treatment that can be applied in a variety of ways with a breadth of clients by providing a general but structured protocol. This will give you a jumping-off point to learn how to do ACT, developing competencies and strategies that you can continue to adapt and flexibly apply, based on your understanding of ACT, clinical style, setting, and clients. Before we go into how to do ACT, we will define what ACT is within the broader evidence-based therapy field. In a sense, this foundation of what ACT is will help you grasp how the engine of ACT works, so when potential issues arise (e.g., how to respond when a client does X), you will have the prerequisite knowledge to steer your therapy session effectively while staying consistent with the ACT model.

ACT IS PART OF THE CBT TRADITION

ACT is a modern form of CBT. Readers may be familiar with debates in the early 2000s regarding how ACT overlaps, versus is distinct from, other existing CBT approaches (e.g., Hayes, 2004; Hayes et al., 2013; Hofmann & Asmundson, 2008). Part of this grew out of attempts to define a "third wave" of modern CBTs that included ACT among other newer CBTs that incorporated mindfulness and acceptance procedures, often with a behavior analytic foundation (e.g., dialectical behavior therapy, functional analytic psychotherapy, modern forms of behavioral activation; Hayes, 2004). This led some to question whether treatments like ACT represented something new and different within CBT and how it was situated within the broader field. However, as of 2020, these discussions are largely historical and the relation between ACT and traditional CBT has been partially clarified.

In broad strokes, ACT can be understood as being part of the CBT tradition that includes an integration of behavior therapy and its underlying basic behavioral science (i.e., respondent and operant conditioning) with modern scientific accounts that further address the role of internal processes such as cognitions and emotions. Like other forms of CBT, ACT recognizes that an adequate approach to treating clients has to include an account that not only leverages what we know about human behavior and how to influence it but also addresses the complex interplay of cognitions, emotions, and other internal factors that influence our actions and experiences.

ACT also overlaps with defining aspects of CBT, including imposing general parameters for treatment that give it structure amidst flexibility in its application. These parameters include (1) focusing treatment on collaboratively developed clinical targets and goals within a sensitive time period (i.e., treatment is time-limited and appropriate to clinical needs), (2) being guided by ongoing assessment and tracking of client functioning, and (3) being driven by a case conceptualization that is continually updated. ACT differs from other CBTs in terms of the degree of rigid adherence to protocols that are necessary and sufficient for defining a treatment (i.e., fidelity to protocols). However, as this book shows, ACT *can* be implemented with a protocol that includes parameters around the number, focus, and content of sessions. ACT is just more flexible in terms of the degree to which a protocol is needed and the degree of flexibility within a protocol.

That said, ACT also differs from other forms of CBT as it has traditionally been practiced and taught. Most often, these differences between ACT and traditional CBT are discussed in terms of how ACT conceptualizes and addresses clients' internal experiences (Hayes, 2004). For example, some forms of CBT might seek to reduce and replace anxious thoughts that lead to avoiding feared situations so a client can approach these situations *because* the thoughts have changed (i.e., changing thoughts to change actions). In contrast, ACT would seek to reduce the effect of anxious thoughts on one's behavior so that feared situations are approached *despite* having these thoughts (i.e., reducing the impact of thoughts on actions). Before we go into how these differences affect clinical approach, it is worth exploring the deeper philosophical differences between traditional CBT and ACT in how human behavior is studied, conceptualized, and addressed (Hayes et al., 2013).

FUNCTIONAL CONTEXTUALISM AS THE FOUNDATION FOR ACT

ACT is based on a philosophy of science called "functional contextualism" (Hayes, Hayes, & Reese, 1988), which provides the foundation for how we develop and organize our knowledge about human behavior. Although this can feel esoteric at times, by the time you finish this section, we hope we will have made a good case for why this understanding matters and how it can be useful to your learning ACT. These functional contextual assumptions provide the building blocks for the treatment strategies you will learn throughout this book.

Behavior-in-context as the unit of analysis

A defining feature of functional contextualism is its focus on understanding behavior *in context*. If we think of *behavior* as anything a person does (including thoughts, feelings, and other events we cannot see), *context* refers to everything else external to that in terms of situation (time, location, other people's reaction, etc.) and history (what has happened in the past before and after the given behavior). From a functional contextual perspective, we can only understand a given action if we include context. For example, the thought "I'm worthless" cannot be removed and studied in isolation. We have to understand it by looking at when the thought comes up, what the person's history with the thought is, and what happens after the thought occurs.

This might still feel like intellectual jargon, but it echoes down into how thoughts are treated in ACT. There are not rational thoughts that are healthy and irrational thoughts that need to be changed to support healthy functioning. Rather, these are all just behaviors occurring in specific contexts. Someone might have the thought "I'm worthless" after waving at another person who does not reciprocate. This person might have a rich history of believing and treating this thought as factually true, as well as a history of important loved ones telling them they are "worthless." This history might lead to withdrawing from others out of shame for being truly "worthless," which in the past has led to successfully escaping these feelings of shame for a brief period of time. From a functional contextual perspective, there is a lot to "I'm worthless" that has to do with these contextual factors (i.e., what happens around this thought currently and in the past). These contextual factors help us understand how "I'm worthless" functions and how we might change these behaviors to support healthier functioning. For example, we could try to reduce the frequency of the thought by targeting the contexts in which it occurs (e.g., avoiding awkward hand waves, only waving at people they know can see them), change the content of the thought by teaching other ways of thinking in those situations (e.g., identifying other reasons someone might not wave back), or change the function of the thought by changing how one relates to it (e.g., noticing it as just a thought). At its core, the idea is that we do not fully understand any given behavior (including inner experiences like thoughts and feelings) until we know the current and historical context.

Prediction *and* influence is the goal

This leads to the second key feature of functional contextualism: its emphasis on not only predicting but also influencing (i.e., changing) behavior. We can only say we understand a behavior if we can both predict and influence it.

Often in psychology we focus on building strong predictive models that represent the world as it "truly is" in an effort to understand human behavior. For example, we might try to build a model that identifies the mechanisms that predict depressive episodes (i.e., what causes depression). This might have a pragmatic goal underneath it, such as "if we really understand what causes depression, then we can treat and prevent depression." But the whole approach is about prediction with an assumption that the ability to influence depression will naturally follow.

What is cool about functional contextualism is the idea that we might approach the whole enterprise of understanding human behavior and building up to applied theories with a deep commitment to changing behavior, not just predicting it. The goal is not to model a world as it truly is, but to model a world that gives us the ability to predict and influence behavior reliably. Sometimes those models overlap, but not always. Instead, theoretical concepts and principles ultimately are treated simply as "ways of speaking" that aim to carve up the world in whatever ways aid prediction *and* influence. An analysis is true insofar as it is useful in telling us how to predict when the behavior will occur and influence the behavior. This allows us to build and discard concepts on the basis of how well they serve these goals—not haphazardly, but in a rigorous way of knowledge building.

For example, the flexible functional approach to ACT is deeply rooted in a pragmatic approach to understanding behavior—whatever works to predict and influence behavior. There is no "right" way to do ACT. Instead, ACT orients to a set of therapeutic processes that reliably predict and influence behavior, and whatever works to move those processes is functionally doing ACT. Similarly, we encourage you to focus on workability with your clients; there is no right or wrong way to live their lives, but we can help them identify what is not working and find what works well, based on what they want for themselves.

Successful working is the goal

This brings in another interesting aspect of functional contextualism, which is the need to state the goal we are working toward so we can evaluate success. In science, we use prediction and influence, but with clients we need more precision in terms of what they are working for. In this way, the values work in ACT really echoes from these functional contextual roots in terms of identifying the criterion for what works with the client and using that as a touchstone to figure out how well things are going in therapy. If a given ACT strategy does not help a client move toward what matters to them, then it does not work and should be discarded to try something new. This is part of what we really like about ACT and what makes us passionate to teach it to others. Ultimately, it puts the client in the driver's seat to find and build on what is going to work to live a meaningful life in line with what deeply matters to them.

THE BEHAVIOR ANALYTIC AND COGNITIVE ROOTS OF ACT

ACT is rooted within behavior analysis, and in many ways functional contextualism simply explicates the underlying assumptions and philosophy of at least a primary wing of behavior analysis (Hayes et al., 1988). ACT uses behavior analytic principles and methods, which provide basic analytic units for understanding reliable relations between context and behavior that can be used to predict and influence behavior. This again is reflected in ACT, with an emphasis on understanding behavior in context for assessment, case conceptualization, and intervention. Many of the ACT concepts and methods you will learn are direct or indirect reflections of traditional behavior analysis and its extensions into clinical work.

That said, ACT diverges from traditional behavior analysis in an important area that is also reflected in the divergence that was found when CBT emerged from traditional behavior therapy. During the 1970s, therapists were increasingly becoming disillusioned with the limitations of traditional (first-wave) behavior therapy for problems clients routinely presented with and were embracing cognitive therapy approaches pioneered by leaders such as Aaron Beck, Albert Ellis, and Jack Rachman, which influenced CBT as we know it today. Although behavior analysis included a progressive scientific account of internal experiences including cognitions, pioneered by B. F. Skinner, this behavior analytic account was limited when extended to more complex human phenomena typically encountered in therapeutic work. Thus, just like cognitive therapists who shifted from behavior therapy to CBT because they needed a more comprehensive account of cognition, early ACT development led by Steven Hayes faced a challenge in addressing cognition with the available behavior analytic tools (Zettle, 2005). This led to the development of relational frame theory (RFT; Hayes, Barnes-Holmes, & Roche, 2001), a modern behavior analytic account of cognition that informs approaches like ACT to address the complexities of behavior enacted by verbal animals.

Thus, in some ways, ACT ended up in a similar place as traditional CBT, with a melding of a traditional behavioral approach with more modern accounts of cognition. But the pathway ACT took was different and resulted in a quite distinct foundation and set of analytic tools—defined by functional contextualism and RFT (Hayes et al, 2013).

We will take a moment here to explain RFT a bit to show how this distinct behavior analytic account of cognition has substantial implications for how clinical problems are conceptualized and treated in ACT. The core of RFT is that verbal humans have the ability to relate things to each other—even relations that are not immediately obvious and that have never been learned before—and these relations can alter how these things function or the effect they have on individuals. By "relations" we mean all the ways we might describe how one stimulus is similar to, different from, bigger or smaller than, a part of, contingent on, or otherwise associated with another stimulus. These relations are the "glue" that hold together many complex ideas and rules for behavior that can be adaptive or maladaptive (e.g.,

"Having one drink is a relapse, and if I relapse then I'm a failure, and if I failed, I might as well keep drinking."). What makes RFT so innovative and important for ACT is that these ways of relating things have unique features, including (1) we have the ability to derive new relations that have never been learned; (2) coherence (making sense) functions as a reinforcer; (3) changes in functions can occur through derived relations; and (4) these relations and changes in functions are all controlled by context.

The ability to derive new relations

Humans have a unique capacity to relate things in new ways they have never learned before and that may not be immediately obvious. For example, try this right now. How is a toaster similar or different from a dog? It might take a minute because there are no immediate relations you have learned or that are obvious. But given enough time, you could probably derive a relation between the two— they both are essential parts of any good household, they both eat bread if given the chance, one should be on the counter and the other should not, one runs on electricity and the other on treats and love, and so on.

We know from a long series of carefully controlled studies that humans have the ability to derive relations that have never been taught (Hayes et al., 2001). This can work well in some situations, like if you had to figure out how to escape from a dangerous situation you have never been in. Yet, it can also create challenges, like if you thought you had to escape from a situation that is not actually dangerous. Through the process of being able to relate anything to anything else, we have a fantastic ability to evaluate, plan, create, and problem-solve in ways that make our species incredibly successful. However, we also have a fantastic ability to evaluate in unhelpful judgmental ways, to come up with ineffective plans for events that will never occur, to create new ways of making ourselves and others miserable, and to problem-solve things that are either not problems or not solvable. In any moment, we can relate seemingly trivial, neutral things to incredibly aversive, upsetting things, thus greatly expanding our capacity for suffering. For example, we can associate anything with the label "bad," including our bodies, feelings, and thoughts, and such associations can be unhelpful if we then respond to these stimuli accordingly.

Coherence as a reinforcer

The second key feature identified by RFT is that these relations are reinforced by coherence, meaning we relate things that make sense and seem logical. Again, this is a useful cognitive process because it is usually adaptive to think logically and not contradict ourselves. But this also means relating is automatically reinforced by coherence and thus can continue to elicit and strengthen the ongoing behavior without conscious attention. Much like how eating each chip in a bag of chips can be automatically reinforcing and lead to the next chip, we can keep "making sense of things" all day. This might explain the automatic nature and frequency of thinking. We are constantly relating things to each other, seemingly on autopilot, and without much ability to control it. We do not relate things based primarily on what makes us feel good or helps us but rather what makes sense. Consequently, we can get wrapped up in an ongoing stream of a logical story about how we are not good enough, will never be loved, should give up, and so on. Again, as this process is automatic, ACT uses strategies (mindfulness, acceptance) to observe this process and choose when to be regulated by it.

Changes in function

We might be able to relatively easily manage just these two features of relating anything to anything else on an almost constant loop based on what "makes sense," if not for a third feature. The ways we relate things change how these things function. If we were constantly evaluating ourselves and thinking about how we are terrible but it did not change how we felt, acted, or otherwise engaged in the world, it probably would not be a big deal. But in actuality, how we relate (or think about) things affects all these other aspects of our functioning. The thought "I can't handle my anxiety" can transform the discomfort of anxiety into absolute fear as anxiety becomes something dangerous, unmanageable, and to be avoided at all costs. This can not only intensify an event but also change its overall meaning. For example, if being at home on a Friday night is related to "nobody likes me," then watching a movie and relaxing at home can all of a sudden be a sad and lonely activity, despite its being an enjoyable event without that thought.

This is all contextually controlled

Although we can relate anything to anything and thereby change our experiences and reactions to these things, this process is not random. Rather, all these relations and transformations through relations are governed by context. This is why when you see the letters *bat* you do not immediately have all the reactions you would normally have to seeing a disgusting, flying rodent (apologies to bat lovers) as well as to playing baseball. Rather, the symbols associated with *bat* only have meaning in context, such as your history with these symbols, the collection of symbols surrounding it, and the context in which you are interacting with this book. We could say "Get out, there is a fire," but you probably would not run out the house right this moment because of the context. However, you might do that if someone woke you up at 3 A.M. yelling the exact same phrase. Context is extremely important in governing how we relate things and how things change as a result. This is extremely important for ACT as a functional contextual approach because it gives us a way to reduce maladaptive functions and build up more adaptive ones. For example, we can shift the important and sad thought "I'm fat" to "funny sound that shows up in my head" using techniques like acceptance and mindfulness. We can also tie scary or anxiety-provoking events to something meaningful and alter the functions of those emotions (e.g., approach rather than avoid) using values.

HOW PEOPLE GET STUCK: THE PSYCHOLOGICAL INFLEXIBILITY MODEL

Overall, this combination of traditional behavior analysis with the additional insight of RFT provides the principles for developing an applied theoretical model of psychopathology (or a theory for how people get stuck) which we call *psychological inflexibility*. This model orients to how cognitive processes alter direct behavioral contingencies to produce excessive suffering and a lack of meaningful, effective action. Overall, psychological inflexibility refers to rigid patterns of behavior in which actions are excessively guided by internal experiences (e.g., thoughts, feelings, cravings) rather than direct contingencies (what is effective) and values (what is meaningful). These are most exemplified by two processes: cognitive fusion and experiential avoidance.

Cognitive fusion describes responding to thoughts in a literal context or as if they were absolutely true. A fused response to "You'll never understand ACT" would be one that treats this as reflecting reality and thus guiding your experiences and behavior. Maybe you will feel sad or anxious and choose to put this book away, never to be opened again. In other words, cognitive fusion means thoughts "push us around" and we do whatever they tell us to do. Similarly, a client who is fused with the thought "There's no point in trying" might give up on an important goal or activity, like quitting smoking, applying for a new job, and so on. Irrespective of how accurate the thought is, the issue is behavior is dominated by thoughts rather than other sources of information.

Experiential avoidance refers to rigid attempts to avoid, get rid of, control, or otherwise change inner experiences (e.g., thoughts, feelings, bodily sensations). This can take many forms because experiential avoidance is defined by the purpose the behavior is intended to serve (regulate inner experiences), not what the behavior looks like. Someone might engage in experiential avoidance by drinking, withdrawing from others, trying to suppress thoughts, cleaning, exercising, practicing mindfulness, or even seeing a therapist. Essentially, if clients are doing a certain behavior to try to get away from an unwanted thought, feeling, or other inner experience, they are engaging in experiential avoidance no matter how "healthy" the behavior looks.

Interestingly, this means either doing what thoughts tell us to do *or* focusing on trying to make thoughts and other inner experiences go away are form of psychological inflexibility that leads to suffering. This makes sense, coming back to context because, in both cases, thoughts, feelings, and other inner experiences are being related to in a literal way, either as true rules that must be followed or as bad, dangerous things that must be avoided. ACT takes the stance that psychological problems are not due to our inner experiences being bad things that must be changed. Rather, many of our problems may be due to how we relate to our experiences, and, more specifically, relating to our experiences as bad, maladaptive things that must be changed may be part of the problem—not the solution.

ACCEPTANCE AND MINDFULNESS AS A PATHWAY TO REDUCE THE IMPACT OF INNER EXPERIENCES

Based on the psychological inflexibility model, clients get stuck when their actions are dominated by their inner experiences and reflect efforts to avoid these experiences. Thus, a large part of ACT is reducing the functional impact of inner experiences by changing how we relate or respond to them. This differs from the default way we typically relate to and try to address inner experiences.

ACT addresses inner experiences through the use of acceptance and mindfulness-based therapeutic procedures. Rather than changing the content of inner experiences, the aim of ACT is to change our relationship to these inner experiences so that they have a weaker impact on behavior. For example, ACT might teach a client to relate to the thought "Everyone thinks I'm weird" as just a thought and to make room for the discomfort of approaching social situations even when difficult thoughts and feelings arise. Rather than inner experiences, ACT targets engagement in meaningful and effective behaviors while being mindful and accepting of inner experiences that arise. When we take this stance, the thought "Everyone thinks I'm weird" does not have to change, because it no longer affects what we do. That is, we can still go to social gatherings and ask people out with the thought "Everyone think I'm weird" present because we have learned to relate to it as just a thought rather than something literally true that must be acted on, fought with, or otherwise treated as a real thing. We typically break these methods down into four core components: cognitive defusion, acceptance, being present, and a flexible sense of self (or self-as-context).

Cognitive defusion is the process of noticing thoughts as just thoughts. It most directly targets its inverse, cognitive fusion. Going back to RFT, this is all about changing the context in which we are responding to inner experiences, such as thoughts. Cognitive defusion helps shift from a literal context where thoughts are true and have power and meaning to one in which thoughts are noticed as just thoughts. For example, we might help a client see a thought as just a bunch of funny symbols on a piece of paper, arbitrary sounds when said out loud, history of which they can recall past occurrences, as a character from a favorite TV show, or even an overeager assistant trying to do its best to help out. The idea is to emphasize other ways our mind works besides the specific one we typically operate on, which is the literal content of what a thought is saying.

Acceptance involves being open and welcoming to unwanted thoughts and feelings and allowing them to be present for what they are without giving into or trying to make them go away. This most directly targets its inverse, experiential avoidance. Initially, acceptance might seem to just be the act of *not* engaging in experiential avoidance: allowing these inner experiences to come and go without efforts to avoid or change them. However, this would miss the more active ways in which acceptance is practiced. Acceptance is more than a lack of fighting; it is an intentional, active, and open stance. That is, we choose to make space for difficult thoughts and feelings rather than feel resigned to their occurrence. Acceptance is more akin to graciously receiving a gift from a loved one than to being hit in the face by an unruly wave.

This is predicated on clients' recognizing these experiences for what they are, thereby creating a context in which thoughts and feelings can be treated as natural reactions instead of things to be avoided or acted on. We emphasize the welcoming stance in acceptance, partly to avoid misinterpreting acceptance as a "just do it" stance where clients are supposed to white-knuckle their way through previously avoided situations while trying to ignore unwanted thoughts and feelings. This can work for a short period, but you would not be doing something radically different with your inner world, and it typically does not work over time as resources and motivation for the effort it takes dwindle. Instead, acceptance means an active, welcoming, mindful approach to inner experiences.

Being present refers to being attentive to relevant experiences and information in the moment in a flexible, effective way. An aspect of psychological inflexibility is the tendency to get stuck with attention rigidly focused on the past or future (e.g., regrets, worries) or to be overly fixated or hypervigilant toward a limited set of experiences in the present (e.g., changes in heart rate, potentially disapproving expressions from others). The aim of ACT is to help clients attend to what is happening in the here-and-now so that behavior can be sensitive to and guided by their current environment—both internal and external. This is another way of reducing the impact of thoughts and feelings as clients attend to a variety of sources of information rather than just their inner world. For example, being present could help a client break out of a mindless eating pattern so they can savor food they enjoy and notice signals that they are full, rather than continuing to overeat on autopilot while they think about their stressors.

Flexible sense of self refers to a process in which clients learn to take a perspective in which the "self" is more than, distinct from, and the container of their inner experiences (a process we also sometimes call *self-as-context* in ACT). Due to the inherently abstract nature of this process, it is often best understood through experiential exercises and metaphors. For example, imagine you are the sky and your thoughts and feelings are the passing clouds and weather. In other words, you are a stable, broad perspective that can simply observe the passing inner experiences. Just like how the sky cannot be defined by or threatened by the weather, you cannot be defined by or threatened by your thoughts and feelings. This observing self-perspective can help break unhelpful patterns when clients are overly entangled with a "self-story" about who they are, what they should do, what is wrong with them, and so on because the "self" becomes no longer tied to these narratives. Instead, the "self" is perceived as a dispassionate, observing entity through which thoughts and feelings occur. This self-perspective can also strengthen other acceptance and mindfulness processes. It becomes easier to acknowledge and allow experiences to be present for what they are when we can see them as a part of ourselves, rather than as who we are.

The combination of cognitive defusion, acceptance, being present, and a flexible sense of self can be conceptualized as the mindfulness components of ACT. These processes overlap in many ways with conceptualizations of mindfulness as a way of attending to the present in a nonreactive, accepting way. One of the things we like about the ACT approach to these mindfulness processes is that it orients to functional processes that you can engage in various ways with clients outside of typical mindfulness meditation strategies. For example, you can elicit, model, and reinforce these processes in conversations with your client. If a client said in session, "I'm really anxious about this upcoming family party," a therapist could give a response supporting defusion ("So your mind is saying this could go really bad and is giving many thoughts about what might go wrong."), or acceptance ("So anxiety is present right now, can we just make space for that to be here?"), or being present ("What are you noticing right now as this anxiety comes up?"), or a flexible sense of self ("Imagine you were at the party right now. What other experiences might you notice passing by like clouds from that 'sky' perspective we discussed?"). Echoing back to the pragmatic goal of whatever works to predict and influence behavior, these therapeutic processes can orient therapists to multiple approaches to change client behavior and provide considerable flexibility in how these goals are achieved.

Although these processes largely have the aim of changing the context in which we relate to our thoughts and feelings, they ultimately are used to seek to change what clients do so they are better able to engage in meaningful actions. The goal is not to notice or accept painful psychological experiences for their own sake; it is to empower clients to do what matters even when difficult thoughts and feelings arise. Thus, this work should not end with clients simply doing something "between their ears" but with changing overt behavior. If these mindfulness methods work, we should see changes in behavior. As maladaptive effects of inner experiences on behavior are lessened, clients will have more opportunity to act on the basis of what would be meaningful or effective in the moment.

VALUES AND COMMITTED ACTION AS A PATHWAY TO DOING WHAT MATTERS

Again, the ultimate goal of ACT is not to change unwanted inner experiences; it is to empower clients to live fulfilling lives. That is, the aim of ACT is to help clients do what matters to them. Thus, lessening the impact of inner experiences on clients' actions is done in the service of helping clients identify and engage in meaningful activities. As unhelpful guides for action are reduced (e.g., cognitive fusion, experiential avoidance), clients often need help figuring out what they want to be doing and how to actually do it. This is addressed with the values and committed action components of ACT.

Values refers to what is deeply important to clients in terms of how they act and what their actions stand for. We all have things that are important to us and that we would work toward. Sometimes we develop these values individually, and sometimes they are largely culturally based. Regardless of their sources, they function as reinforcers. One way to clarify this is to consider an ordinary action like cooking. You can approach cooking in various ways. For example, you could cook in a way that is creative, fun, connected with other people, giving a sense of purpose and meaning to the activity. However, you could also cook in a way that is mindless, rushed, or resentful. Depending on your stance toward the task, your experience of the same action will likely differ. Thus, actively connecting with our values in the moment can change how we experience our behaviors, making them more fulfilling to us. In other words, values are found in *how* actions are taken, focusing on the qualities people bring to actions rather than the outcome (whether the meal is delicious or others like it). This is a cognitive process in that clients are asked to describe more abstract principles that can guide and motivate their actions across a range of situations. This is an example of how ACT· uses RFT to clients' advantage: by using cognitions—or our verbal ability to associate anything with anything—to increase effective patterns of behavior and reduce unhelpful effects of cognition on behavior. As you will see in later chapters, ACT uses various strategies to help clients identify their values and learn how to use these values to motivate doing what matters to them.

Committed action refers to the doing part of this work, helping clients build larger and larger patterns of meaningful activity in their lives. In many ways, this is where the "rubber meets the road" with everything done in ACT as clients practice acceptance and mindfulness to move toward their values with specific behavioral commitments. This might fit in well with other behavior change work you have done in which you set specific goals with your clients for what they will do to make meaningful changes and practice what they have learned in therapy. Committed action includes goal setting and sometimes behavioral methods that help ensure that clients are successful in following through with their goal (e.g., behavioral activation, exposure). Committed action is also where other behavioral methods might be integrated to teach clients how to do new things if there is a skills deficit (e.g., social skills training). Lastly, we use committed action as a way to orient to ongoing therapy goals and relapse prevention from an ACT perspective focusing on building patterns of valued activity over time and returning to commitments when clients go off course.

THIS ALL LEADS TO PSYCHOLOGICAL FLEXIBILITY

Altogether, this combination of acceptance, mindfulness, and values-based processes is referred to as the *psychological flexibility model*, which is the ACT model for psychological health and therapeutic change. Thus, psychological flexibility refers to the ability to engage in meaningful actions while being mindful and accepting of whatever inner experiences arise—in other words, to be able to do what matters while being open and aware to whatever the present moment affords, including unwanted thoughts and feelings. The hexaflex graphic is commonly used to display this model (see Figure 1.1), which highlights how each of the processes we have discussed are part of psychological flexibility and interconnected. For example, being able to notice thoughts as just thoughts (cognitive defusion) is predicated on attending to thoughts (being present), which can then help facilitate accepting difficult thoughts (acceptance) and doing what matters (values, committed actions). Overall, psychological flexibility is the solution to getting stuck in psychological inflexibility.

This psychological flexibility model provides a guide for how to conceptualize cases and practice ACT with your clients. For example, some clients may struggle more with targets on the left side of the hexaflex, by being caught up in thoughts or being avoidant, while others might struggle more with the right side, by not knowing what matters to them or not knowing skills deficits in being able to act effectively. Similarly, you might notice different processes at play in any moment (e.g., a client being on autopilot and disconnected with values) and points at

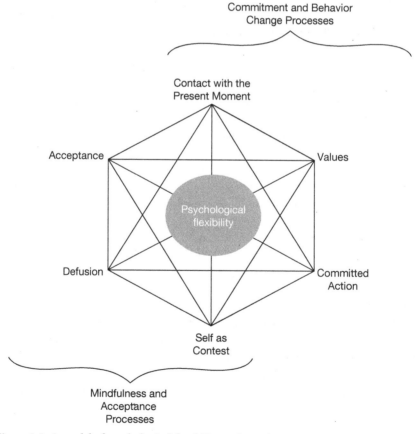

Figure 1.1 A model of psychological flexibility and its subprocesses.

which you will have to choose what process to leverage (e.g., should I lean in on attending to the present moment or explore their values?).

The psychological flexibility model orients back to where we started in this chapter: ACT is defined functionally in terms of a set of therapeutic processes designed to help clients get unstuck from patterns that prevent them from doing what matters in their lives. Psychological inflexibility can manifest differently across individuals. Hence, the focus is on the function of behaviors (i.e., actions that are overly guided by literal interpretations of thoughts or avoiding unwanted inner experiences). These functions can underlie a wide range of clinical presentations and problem behaviors with which you might work—wherever people can get stuck in unhelpful ways of relating to their inner experiences. This also means ACT can be applied across this breadth of clinical presentations to reduce psychological inflexibility by increasing psychological flexibility.

APPLYING THE PSYCHOLOGICAL FLEXIBILITY MODEL: DOING ACT

A focus on function over form not only expands the variety of clients to whom ACT can be applied, it also expands the variety of ways a therapist can increase psychological flexibility. ACT is not defined by any technique or specific form of behavior on the part of the therapist; what matters is that the therapist has a functional impact on their client that increases psychological flexibility. This means you can fit ACT to your personal style, skills, and setting, taking your existing strengths and applying them to the psychological flexibility model.

That said, this can also be a challenge for therapists new to ACT. There are countless ways to implement ACT with your clients, and trainings in ACT regularly focus more on the function and flexibility with which ACT can be implemented. This can sometimes make it hard for therapists learning ACT to know what to do in the moment with clients, how to stick to ACT rather than fall back into other treatments they already know, and how to build on areas in which they have less competence.

In this book, we will focus on one way to do ACT. That is all it is: one way among many to use the psychological flexibility model. We hope to provide a set of stepping stones you can use to begin your journey with learning ACT. You can follow the protocol in this book for an initial set of cases, using the structure and scaffolding to learn the basics. As you practice this protocol, you will hopefully get a better sense of what it looks like to do ACT in the moment, how to identify the target functions in ACT in session, and some key ACT strategies. We hope this gives you a basic foundation you can build on and integrate into your therapeutic style and orientation as you continue to explore the exciting and broad opportunities that ACT provides in working with clients to make meaningful changes in their lives.

REFERENCES

Association for Contextual Behavioral Science. (2020). ACT randomized controlled trials since 1986. Retrieved from https://contextualscience.org/ACT_Randomized_Controlled_Trials

A-Tjak, J. G. L., Davis, M. L., Morina, N., Powers, M. B., Smits, J. A. J., & Emmelkamp P. M. G. (2015). A meta-analysis of the efficacy of acceptance and commitment therapy for clinically relevant mental and physical health problems. *Psychotherapy and Psychosomatics, 84*(30), 30–36.

Bluett, E. J., Homan, K. J., Morrison, K. L., Levin, M. E., & Twohig, M. P. (2014). Acceptance and commitment therapy for anxiety and OCD spectrum disorders: An empirical review. *Journal of Anxiety Disorders, 6,* 612–624.

Hayes, S. C. (2004). Acceptance and commitment therapy, relational frame theory, and the third wave of behavior therapy. *Behavior Therapy, 35,* 639–665.

Hayes, S. C., Barnes-Holmes, D., & Roche, B. (Eds.). (2001). *Relational frame theory: A post-Skinnerian account of human language and cognition.* Kluwer Academic/Plenum Publishers.

Hayes, S. C., Hayes, L. J., & Reese, H. W. (1988). Finding the philosophical core: A review of Stephen C. Pepper's world hypotheses: A study in evidence. *Journal of the Experimental Analysis of Behavior, 50,* 97.

Hayes, S. C., Levin, M. E., Plumb-Vilardaga, J., Villatte, J. L., & Pistorello, J. (2013). Acceptance and commitment therapy and contextual behavioral science: Examining the progress of a distinctive model of behavioral and cognitive therapy. *Behavior Therapy, 44*(2), 180–198.

Hofmann, S. G., & Asmundson, G. J. G. (2008). Acceptance and mindfulness-based therapy: New wave or old hat? *Clinical Psychology Review, 28,* 1–16.

Hughes, L. S., Clark, J., Colclough, J. A., Dale, E., & McMillan, D. (2017). Acceptance and commitment therapy (ACT) for chronic pain: A systematic review and meta-analyses. *Clinical Journal of Pain, 33,* 552–568.

Lee, E. B., An, W., Levin, M. E., & Twohig, M. P. (2015). An initial meta-analysis of acceptance and commitment therapy for treating substance use disorders. *Drug and Alcohol Dependence, 155,* 1–7.

Twohig, M. P., & Levin M. E. (2017). Acceptance and commitment therapy as a treatment for anxiety and depression: A review. *Psychiatric Clinics, 40,* 751–770.

Zettle, R. D. (2005). The evolution of a contextual approach to therapy: From comprehensive distancing to ACT. *International Journal of Behavioral Consultation and Therapy, 1,* 77–89.

Assessment

ACT is a function-based treatment, which means therapeutic choices depend on the purpose or meaning that client behaviors serve in context. No thought, feeling, or bodily sensation is inherently good or bad. To understand these experiences and behaviors, we have to know more than their form. In ACT, we look at how that inner experience affects the client and what actions it likely leads to. Similarly, we look at the meaning behind actions more so than the behaviors themselves. In ACT, we may target a diagnosable disorder, but at other times we might heavily focus on growing meaningful patterns of behavior. ACT is person-centered, and people are unique and complicated. Therefore, you will need to know your client's current clinical presentation and life situation in order to make the best treatment plans. While many areas of assessment need to occur, we are going to orient you to four basic areas which should prepare you to implement ACT. Some of what we will discuss provides guidance for general assessment, and some of it is specific to ACT. The following is not a comprehensive guide for assessment. Instead, we focus on variables that might help you determine if ACT is a good fit for your client, and help you implement ACT more effectively in subsequent sessions.

FOUR MAIN AREAS OF ASSESSMENT FROM AN ACT APPROACH

1. Determine the primary clinical concern(s). That is, what is the client seeking services for?
2. Determine the functional context maintaining the target behaviors.
3. Assess for contextual, historical, or cultural variables that play into the case presentation.
4. Set up an ongoing assessment program for treatment.

1. Determine the primary clinical concern(s)

This statement probably seems obvious to individuals working from an empirically supported treatment- or evidence-based practice approach, because such interventions largely target specific disorders or clinical issues. Condition-specific interventions aimed at symptom reduction contrast with treatments focused on a broader underlying or intrapsychic issue. While ACT targets an underlying process that manifests as a clinical issue, its ultimate goal is to create a different behavioral pattern by the end of treatment.

Some of your clients will have received therapy or be otherwise well-versed in psychology and know that therapy tends to focus on a particular set of issues. For instance, someone who is being treated in the Veterans Administration (VA) system will likely know their diagnoses and even know which ones or what elements of them they want help with. However, other clients may know very little about what is occurring for them and be looking for guidance from the therapist. Personally, we think having an objective treatment target is helpful to the client. Having a predetermined goal or target allows the client and therapist to judge the utility of sessions objectively, as it provides a clear metric for success.

As an example, a client may enter therapy because life is difficult and they feel depressed. After a thorough assessment, you determine that the client meets criteria for social anxiety disorder and major depressive disorder—with the depression secondary to the anxiety disorder. Additionally, both issues are affecting the individual's college education, job satisfaction, as well as romantic and other social relationships. Finally, all these disorders are occurring in a social and cultural context that makes change difficult (e.g., sexism or racism), along with financial limitations and skills deficits with regard to higher education, and so on. All this information should be shared with the client, and a collaborative decision about goals should be made.

We suggest targeting the clinical issue that will have the most positive effect on the client's life and affect other clinical issues. Often, one clinical issue will affect other ones; for example, lessening social anxiety will most likely lessen the feeling of depression. Similarly, if social anxiety is lessened, then school and other social struggles will likely diminish, which will also affect depression. While this all may seem obvious to the therapist, this logic should be discussed with the client. One limitation to this approach is that it parses a whole client into actions or disorders rather than addressing all the aspects of the client's life.

While a holistic approach has clear advantages, we see multiple, distinct, positive features to targeting one particular issue—especially for people learning a therapy. First, anyone who has done a lot of therapy knows how it can become about the "problem of the week" unless there is some decent guidance for the sessions. Each week the client may have a new struggle, and the therapist can easily assist in addressing that issue. A talented ACT therapist could keep coming back to the six processes of change and how they play into these weekly issues, but actively building on a solid skill foundation is more difficult, as the situations are different each week. Alternatively, if the client and therapist agree on a particular issue to work on, every session can focus on that clinical issue. Therefore, the sessions are more structured. This also helps the client to come out of therapy with gains in at least one area.

Second, studies generally show that targeting one area with ACT will affect other clinical issues (Morrison et al., 2019; Ong et al., 2019). Personally, we have seen many clients with whom we targeted a specific diagnosable issue and observed notable change in that issue throughout treatment. Then, toward the end of therapy, as positive changes occurred in their main area of concern, clients started working on other less immediate issues. We see this as partially being the result of individuals' dealing with the most pressing issues in life before moving on to other things. Another element is that they have likely developed psychological flexibility—including more values clarity—and are now able to follow those values more easily and generalize the skills to different life domains.

Third, and maybe most important for the purpose of this book, having one clear target gives direction to the therapist and client. The therapist can focus on conceptualizing and addressing the main clinical presentation. The target private event stays the same throughout treatment, overt and covert avoidance actions are clearer, and how the client's actions tie into values remains consistent. This allows the client and therapist to work from a straightforward conceptualization throughout treatment rather than shifting the case conceptualization at each session. If more sessions are indicated at the end of therapy, the therapist and client can agree to add more. In our experience, if a client comes in with a concern, the sessions focus on that concern, and there is some success with it, the client will happily end therapy. Even though there may be unlimited issues for which we can see therapists, we generally only do so when these issues reach a notable level of concern. However, we do not typically seek additional assistance until that happens.

To summarize, we recommend engaging in a full assessment and determining all clinical issues that the client is dealing with. Next, we recommend working with the client to determine what the main clinical issue is and making that the focus of therapy. After that main clinical issue is lessened, the therapist can check back on the other ones and see what the client would like to do about them. It is likely the secondary and tertiary clinical issues will also have decreased such that the client is no longer concerned with them and will want to end therapy.

2. Determine the functional context maintaining the target behavior

The issue with assessments based on diagnosis is that they miss the idiographic elements of each clinical presentation, given there are many ways similar diagnoses can be initiated or maintained. This is not always detrimental to therapy, because many manualized treatments are robust enough to handle different functions of similar presentations. In this segment of assessment, we aim to do three things: (1)

AAQ-II

Below you will find a list of statements. Please rate how true each statement is for you by circling a number next to it. Use the scale below to make your choice.

1	2	3	4	5	6	7
never true	very seldom true	seldom true	sometimes true	frequently true	almost always true	always true

1. My painful experiences and memories make it difficult for me to live a life that i would value.	1 2 3 4 5 6 7
2. I'm afraid of my feelings.	1 2 3 4 5 6 7
3. I worry about not being able to control my worries and feelings.	1 2 3 4 5 6 7
4. My painful memories prevent me from having a fulfilling life.	1 2 3 4 5 6 7
5. Emotions cause problems in my life.	1 2 3 4 5 6 7
6. It seems like most people are handling their lives better than I am.	1 2 3 4 5 6 7
7. Worries get in the way of my success.	1 2 3 4 5 6 7

Figure 2.1 The Acceptance and Action Questionnaire—II. Sum item ratings to obtain a total scale score. Higher scores indicate more psychological inflexibility.

determine if the clinical presentation is largely the result of psychological inflexibility; (2) if it is, dig deeper into what elements of psychological inflexibility contribute to the clinical issue; and (3) identify other clinical variables that might be a part of the presentation (e.g., social skills deficit, strained family relations).

It is easy to determine if psychological inflexibility plays a role in the clinical issue by giving the client the Acceptance and Action Questionnaire–II (AAQ-II; Bond et al., 2011), a general measure of psychological inflexibility. We have included a copy of the AAQ-II here as it is not copyrighted (see Figure 2.1). Scores range from 7 to 49, with higher scores indicating more psychological inflexibility (i.e., high is bad, low is good). Generally, a score over 24 is considered to be in the clinical range, although these cutoffs vary depending on the presentation and demographic profile of the client. This measure can be slow to move, so there is no reason to give it more often than every other session. As noted, the AAQ-II is a general psychological inflexibility measure and specific versions of the AAQ have been created for particular disorders. The context-specific AAQs generally function better and are more sensitive to changes as a result of therapy. A list of them (as of the writing of this book) is provided in Table 2.1. The AAQ will only give you general data on whether your client struggles with psychological inflexibility; client-specific assessment materials and questions can help you really learn what is happening for your client.

If you believe psychological inflexibility is a significant variable in the clinical presentation, we suggest exploring which aspects of psychological inflexibility are most relevant. There are a few ways to evaluate client psychological inflexibility. In our opinion, they are functionally quite similar: They orient you toward the six processes of change as they pertain to your client. One of our favorites, and the one we use in our graduate program training, is the ACT ADVISOR (see Figure 2.2), which was originally created by David Chantry and openly distributed via the Web. We like the version provided in this book because it has simple reminders of what each process is and shows each process on a continuum. It is important to remember that each of these six processes is functional, which means where one wants to be on the continuum depends on context. In our clinical work, we complete this at the beginning of therapy and then every few sessions throughout. It helps us know which of the six processes of change we should be focusing on.

We assess for each of these processes by quickly interviewing the client at the beginning of a therapy session or by putting information together from other conversations. As you get to know your client, it becomes easier to know where they stand on each of these six processes. Remember, where your clients are with respect to these processes varies depending on the situation, so you may need to either find an average of where they are or think in terms of the most pertinent situations for each of these processes (e.g., work, romantic relationships).

Here are examples of questions you can ask to get a sense of where people are on the six processes. We will use anxiety as the example to make the questions clearer, but you can adjust them based on your client's presenting concern.

Acceptance
How do you usually respond to anxiety when it is there?
Are you OK with feeling anxiety?
Do you generally allow anxiety to be there, or do you push it away?

Defusion
When anxiety shows up, how does it affect you?
Is anxiety easy or difficult to feel?
What are your feelings toward anxiety?

Self-as-context
Does your anxiety define you?
Can you see yourself without anxiety?
How would you define yourself?

Being present
Do you think about the present, past, or future most?
When anxiety shows up, do you pay attention to it or other things
    happening around you?
Does your anxiety take you out of the moment?

Values
What are the most important things to you in life?
If anxiety was not in the way, how would you be spending your time?
What do you feel you spend the most time wishing you were doing?

Table 2.1 LIST OF CONTEXT-SPECIFIC PSYCHOLOGICAL FLEXIBILITY MEASURES

Name	Abbreviation	Target Area	Primary Citation	Number of Items
Acceptance and Action Questionnaire— Acquired Brain Injury	AAQ-ABI	Acquired brain injury	Whiting, Deane, Ciarrochi, McLeod, & Simpson (2015)	9
Voices Acceptance and Action Scale	VAAS	Auditory hallucinations (command and/or general)	Shawyer et al. (2007)	31 (command) 12 (general)
Voices Acceptance and Action Scale-9	VAAS-9	Auditory hallucinations (general)	Brockman, Kiernan, & Murrell (2015)	9
Body Image Acceptance and Action Questionnaire	BI-AAQ	Body image (disordered eating focus)	Sandoz, Wilson, Merwin, & Kellum (2013)	12
Body Image Acceptance and Action Questionnaire-5	BI-AAQ-5	Body image (disordered eating focus)	Basarkod, Sahdra, & Ciarrochi (2018)	5
Body Image Psychological Inflexibility Scale	BIPIS	Body image (disturbance and dysmorphia focus)	Callaghan, Sandoz, Darrow, & Feeney (2015)	16
Cancer Acceptance and Action Questionnaire	-	Cancer	Arch & Mitchell (2016)	18
Cardiovascular Disease Acceptance and Action Questionnaire	CVD-AAQ	Cardiovascular disease	Spatola et al. (2014)	7
Experiential Avoidance in Caregiving Questionnaire	EACQ	Caregiving	Losada, Márquez-González, Romero-Moreno, & López (2014)	15
Chronic Illness Acceptance Questionnaire	CIAQ	Chronic illness	Beacham, Linfield, Kinman, & Payne-Murphy (2015)	20
Chronic Pain Acceptance Questionnaire	CPAQ	Chronic pain	McCracken, Vowles, & Eccleston (2004)	20

Table 2.1 Continued

Name	Abbreviation	Target Area	Primary Citation	Number of Items
Chronic Pain Acceptance Questionnaire-8	CPAQ-8	Chronic pain	Fish, McGuire, Hogan, Morrison, & Stewart (2010)	8
Psychological Inflexibility in Pain Scale	PIPS	Chronic pain	Wicksell, Lekander, Sorjonen, & Olsson (2010)	12
Willingness and Acceptance of Delusions Scale	WADS	Delusions	Martins et al. (2018)	12
Acceptance and Action Diabetes Questionnaire	AADQ	Diabetes	Gregg, Callaghan, Hayes, & Glenn-Lawson (2007)	11
Acceptance and Action Epilepsy Questionnaire	AAEpQ	Epilepsy	Lundgren, Dahl, & Hayes (2008)	8
Food Acceptance and Awareness Questionnaire	FAAQ	Food craving	Juarascio, Forman, Timko, Butryn, & Goodwin (2011)	10
Irritable Bowel Syndrome Acceptance and Action Questionnaire	IBSAAQ	Irritable bowel syndrome	Ferreira, Eugenicos, Morris, & Gillanders (2013)	20
Acceptance and Action Questionnaire for Obsessions and Compulsions	AAQ-OC	Obsessions and compulsions	Jacoby, Abramowitz, Buchholz, Reuman, & Blakey (2018)	13
Parental Acceptance and Action Questionnaire	PAAQ	Parenting	Cheron, Ehrenreich, & Pincus (2009)	15
Parenting-Specific Psychological Flexibility	PSPF	Parenting	Brassell et al. (2016)	7
Parental Psychological Flexibility	PPF	Parenting (pre-adolescents and adolescents)	Burke & Moore (2014)	19
Parental Acceptance Questionnaire	6-PAQ	Parents	Greene, Field, Fargo, & Twohig (2015)	18

(continued)

Table 2.1 CONTINUED

Name	Abbreviation	Target Area	Primary Citation	Number of Items
Avoidance and Inflexibility Scale	AIS	Smoking	Gifford, Antonuccio, Kohlenberg, Hayes, & Piasecki (2002)	13
Social Anxiety Acceptance and Action Questionnaire	SA-AAQ	Social anxiety	MacKenzie & Kocovski (2010)	19
Brief Social Anxiety Acceptance and Action Questionnaire	B-SA-AAQ	Social anxiety	MacKenzie et al. (2017)	8
Acceptance and Action Questionnaire— Stigma	AAQ-S	Stigma	Levin, Luoma, Lillis, Hayes, & Vilardaga (2014)	21
Acceptance and Action Questionnaire— Substance Abuse	AAQ-SA	Substance abuse	Luoma, Drake, Kohlenberg, & Hayes (2011)	16
Tinnitus Acceptance Questionnaire	TAQ	Tinnitus	Westin, Hayes, & Andersson (2008)	12
Acceptance and Action Questionnaire for Trichotillomania	AAQ-TTM	Trichotillomania	Houghton et al. (2014)	9
Acceptance and Action Questionnaire for Weight-Related Difficulties	AAQ-W	Weight	Lillis & Hayes (2008)	22
Acceptance and Action Questionnaire for Weight-Related Difficulties Revised	AAQW-R	Weight	Palmeira, Cunha, Pinto-Gouveia, Carvalho, & Lillis (2016)	10
Work-Related Acceptance and Action Questionnaire	WAAQ	Work	Bond, Lloyd, & Guenole (2013)	7

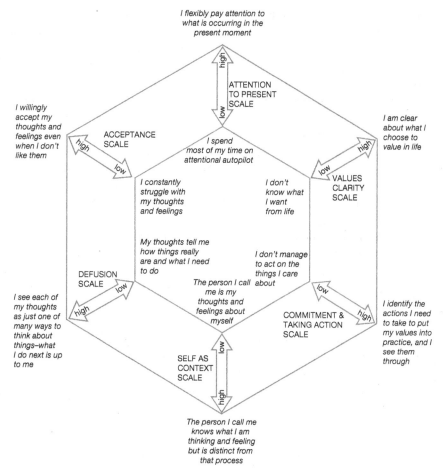

I flexibly pay attention to
what is occurring in the
present moment

ATTENTION TO PRESENT SCALE

high

low

I willingly
accept my
thoughts and
feelings even
when I don't
like them

ACCEPTANCE SCALE

high

low

I spend
most of my time on
attentional autopilot

I am clear
about what I
choose to
value in life

VALUES CLARITY SCALE

high

low

I constantly
struggle with
my thoughts
and feelings

I don't
know what
I want
from life

My thoughts tell me
how things really
are and what I need
to do

DEFUSION SCALE

low

high

I see each of
my thoughts
as just one of
many ways to
think about
things—what
I do next is up
to me

The person I call
me is my
thoughts and
feelings about
myself

I don't manage
to act on the
things I care
about

COMMITMENT & TAKING ACTION SCALE

high

low

I identify the
actions I need
to take to put
my values into
practice, and I
see them
through

SELF AS CONTEXT SCALE

low

high

The person I call me
knows what I am
thinking and feeling
but is distinct from
that process

Figure 2.2 ACT ADVISOR for measuring six processes of psychological flexibility in therapy. Based on the ACT ADVISOR created by David Chantry and modified with permission.

Behavioral commitment

Do you spend more time on what you care about or regulating your
   anxiety?
What do you spend most of your time on?
Does regulating your anxiety take up a lot of your time?

When Hayes, Strosahl, and Wilson (2011) rewrote the original ACT text (Hayes, Strosahl, & Wilson, 1999), they emphasized an "acceptance and mindfulness side" (acceptance, defusion, self-as-context, and being present) and a "values and behavior change side" (values and behavioral commitment). We find this is a useful way to simplify the six processes of change (see Figure 1.1 in Chapter 1).

If the client is caught up in their mind, then they are low on the acceptance and mindfulness side. If they are unaware of what they want and not engaging in meaningful activities, then they are low on the values and behavioral commit-ment side. It can also be useful to think about working on either side rather than on a specific process. We often say to our practicum students, "It looks like you should spend some time on the mindfulness side with that client." Interestingly, if you are working with a client and stuck on one side—meaning you have spent lots of time working on that side with little movement—it might be wise to work on the other side for a while. Sometimes, behavior change is hard because the client is too fused with thoughts or fears what change would entail. Thus, even though behavior change is the place where the client is struggling, the most useful move might be to work on acceptance and defusion before going back to values and behavioral commitments. Alternatively, a client could be unwilling to work on acceptance because they cannot see the reason (or value) behind sitting with discomfort.

In summary, you should assess the role of psychological inflexibility in your client's presentation in two ways. First, have the client complete a standardized as-sessment of psychological flexibility. The AAQ-II is a good option, but we suggest using something context-specific if one is available for your client's presentation. Second, assess the six processes of change at the individual level, which can be guided by a measure like the ACT ADVISOR. If the client is low on psycholog-ical flexibility (high on psychological inflexibility), then ACT is likely an appro-priate treatment. The information from the ACT ADVISOR will tell you which processes need the most attention. Finally, for simplicity, sometimes we lump the six processes of change into two: acceptance and mindfulness, and values and be-havioral commitments.

3. Assess for contextual, historical, or cultural variables that play into the case presentation

Most intake assessments have sections on history, culture, sexual orientation, gender identity, religion, education, family, and so on. We suggest having a list of all the pertinent variables you would want to know about your client. Then, dis-cuss them with your client to see which ones are most meaningful and impactful to them. It is important to know these things, as they influence the way informa-tion is received (e.g., the meaning and function of events) and tells you what your client's most powerful reinforcers will be.

Another way to think of this: Go into the session recognizing that you have never had a client like the one in front of you and that your job is to understand the variables that make this client who they are, which will tell you what type of therapeutic work will be most meaningful to them. For example, if you are working with a client who is religious, ask, "How would changing this behavior affect your spiritual practice?" Similarly, if your client is married and has children, you could ask, "How does having a family affect you?" The key point is to hold preconceptions you may have about your client as hypotheses to be tested through discussions with the client.

4. Set up an ongoing assessment program for treatment

This phase is relatively simple. We encourage finding a main symptomatic measure for your client's presenting issue. If you do not already have this set up in your practice, it will take a little work at the beginning, but once you start to build a file of these different measures, they will be easy to retrieve as you need them. There is a free version of assessment for every diagnosis out there. We highly suggest performing this assessment at baseline, then at whatever frequency makes sense for your client and their presentation (e.g., weekly, every other week), and certainly at the last session. Determining frequency for the assessments can be figured out (1) empirically, by referring to published clinical trials, or (2) using clinical judgment, by considering if the behavior could reasonably change in a week. For example, panic attacks, compulsions, and substance use can change quickly, whereas worry and rumination are likely to be slow to change. We are also fans of having the client track specific actions on a regular basis. For the majority of disorders, there is an overt action that can be tracked. Sometimes it is a proxy variable for the presenting issue. For example, if you are working on depression, you might track bedtime and exercise, whereas you would track amount of substance used for substance use or abuse.

We recommend graphing outcome data along with psychological flexibility scores. If you are not interested in purchasing membership in a Web-based data collection system, you can enter these data into a spreadsheet so that it shows the scores on a graph with clinical and nonclinical means, which can facilitate scoring. Similarly, it can be useful to have additional files containing client total scores so you can easily track outcomes throughout therapy.

REFERENCES

Arch, J. J., & Mitchell, J. L. (2016). An acceptance and commitment therapy (ACT) group intervention for cancer survivors experiencing anxiety at re-entry. *Psychooncology*, 25(5), 610–615. doi:10.1002/pon.3890

Basarkod, G., Sahdra, B., & Ciarrochi, J. (2018). Body Image–Acceptance and Action Questionnaire-5: An abbreviation using genetic algorithms. *Behavior Therapy*, 49(3), 388–402. doi:10.1016/j.beth.2017.09.006

Beacham, A. O., Linfield, K., Kinman, C. R., & Payne-Murphy, J. (2015). The Chronic Illness Acceptance Questionnaire: Confirmatory factor analysis and prediction of perceived disability in an online chronic illness support group sample. *Journal of Contextual Behavioral Science*, 4(2), 96–102. doi:10.1016/j.jcbs.2015.03.001

Bond, F. W., Hayes, S. C., Baer, R. A., Carpenter, K. M., Guenole, N., Orcutt, H. K., . . . Zettle, R. D. (2011). Preliminary psychometric properties of the Acceptance and Action Questionnaire-II: A revised measure of psychological inflexibility and experiential avoidance. *Behavior Therapy*, 42(4), 676–688. doi:10.1016/j.beth.2011.03.007

Bond, F. W., Lloyd, J., & Guenole, N. (2013). The Work-related Acceptance and Action Questionnaire (WAAQ): Initial psychometric findings and their implications for measuring psychological flexibility in specific contexts. *Journal of Occupational and Organizational Psychology, 86*(3), 331–347. doi:10.1111/joop.12001

Brassell, A. A., Rosenberg, E., Parent, J., Rough, J. N., Fondacaro, K., & Seehuus, M. (2016). Parent's psychological flexibility: Associations with parenting and child psychosocial well-being. *Journal of Contextual Behavioral Science, 5*(2), 111–120. doi:10.1016/j.jcbs.2016.03.001

Brockman, R., Kiernan, M., & Murrell, E. (2015). Psychometric properties of two brief versions of the Voices Acceptance and Action Scale (VAAS): Implications for the second-wave and third-wave behavioural and cognitive approaches to auditory hallucinations. *Clinical Psychology & Psychotherapy 22*(5), 450–459. doi:10.1002/cpp.1916

Burke, K., & Moore, S. (2014). Development of the Parental Psychological Flexibility Questionnaire. *Child Psychiatry & Human Development, 46*(4), 548–557. doi:10.1007/s10578-014-0495-x

Callaghan, G. M., Sandoz, E. K., Darrow, S. M., & Feeney, T. K. (2015). The Body Image Psychological Inflexibility Scale: Development and psychometric properties. *Psychiatry Research, 226*(1), 45–52. doi:10.1016/j.psychres.2014.11.039

Cheron, D. M., Ehrenreich, J. T., & Pincus, D. B. (2009). Assessment of parental experiential avoidance in a clinical sample of children with anxiety disorders. *Child Psychiatry & Human Development, 40*(3), 383–403. doi:10.1007/s10578-009-0135-z

Ferreira, N. B., Eugenicos, M. P., Morris, P. G., & Gillanders, D. T. (2013). Measuring acceptance in irritable bowel syndrome: Preliminary validation of an adapted scale and construct utility. *Quality of Life Research, 22*(7), 1761–1766. doi:10.1007/s11136-012-0299-z

Fish, R. A., McGuire, B., Hogan, M., Morrison, T. G., & Stewart, I. (2010). Validation of the Chronic Pain Acceptance Questionnaire (CPAQ) in an internet sample and development and preliminary validation of the CPAQ-8. *Pain, 149*(3), 435–443. doi:10.1016/j.pain.2009.12.016

Gifford, E. V., Antonuccio, D. O., Kohlenberg, B. S., Hayes, S. C., & Piasecki, M. M. (2002). Combining Bupropion SR with acceptance and commitment-based behavioral therapy for smoking cessation: Preliminary results from a randomized controlled trial. Paper presented at the Association for Advancement of Behavioral Therapy, Reno, NV.

Greene, R. L., Field, C. E., Fargo, J. D., & Twohig, M. P. (2015). Development and validation of the parental acceptance questionnaire (6-PAQ). *Journal of Contextual Behavioral Science, 4*(3), 170–175. doi:10.1016/j.jcbs.2015.05.003

Gregg, J. A., Callaghan, G. M., Hayes, S. C., & Glenn-Lawson, J. L. (2007). Improving diabetes self-management through acceptance, mindfulness, and values: A randomized controlled trial. *Journal of Consulting and Clinical Psychology, 75*(2), 336–343. doi:10.1037/0022-006X.75.2.336

Hayes, S. C., Strosahl, K., & Wilson, K. G. (1999). *Acceptance and commitment therapy: An experiential approach to behavior change.* New York: Guilford Press.

Hayes, S. C., Strosahl, K. D., & Wilson, K. G. (2011). *Acceptance and commitment therapy (2nd ed.): The process and practice of mindful change.* New York: Guilford Press.

Houghton, D. C., Compton, S. N., Twohig, M. P., Saunders, S. M., Franklin, M. E., Neal-Barnett, A. M., . . . Woods, D. W. (2014). Measuring the role of psychological inflexibility in trichotillomania. *Psychiatry Research*, *220*(1-2), 356–361. doi:10.1016/j.psychres.2014.08.003

Jacoby, R. J., Abramowitz, J. S., Buchholz, J., Reuman, L., & Blakey, S. M. (2018). Experiential avoidance in the context of obsessions: Development and validation of the Acceptance and Action Questionnaire for Obsessions and Compulsions. *Journal of Obsessive-Compulsive and Related Disorders*, *19*, 34–43. doi:10.1016/j.jocrd.2018.07.003

Juarascio, A., Forman, E., Timko, C. A., Butryn, M., & Goodwin, C. (2011). The development and validation of the Food craving Acceptance and Action Questionnaire (FAAQ). *Eating Behaviors*, *12*(3), 182–187. doi:10.1016/j.eatbeh.2011.04.008

Levin, M. E., Luoma, J. B., Lillis, J., Hayes, S. C., & Vilardaga, R. (2014). The Acceptance and Action Questionnaire–Stigma (AAQ-S): Developing a measure of psychological flexibility with stigmatizing thoughts. *Journal of Contextual Behavioral Science*, *3*(1), 21–26. doi:10.1016/j.jcbs.2013.11.003

Lillis, J., & Hayes, S. C. (2008). Measuring avoidance and inflexibility in weight related problems. *International Journal of Behavioral Consultation and Therapy*, *4*(1), 30–40. doi:10.1037/h0100865

Losada, A., Márquez-González, M., Romero-Moreno, R., & López, J. (2014). Development and validation of the Experiential Avoidance in Caregiving Questionnaire (EACQ). *Aging Mental Health*, *18*(7), 897–904. doi:10.1080/13607863.2014.896868

Lundgren, T., Dahl, J., & Hayes, S. C. (2008). Evaluation of mediators of change in the treatment of epilepsy with acceptance and commitment therapy. *Journal of Behavioral Medicine*, *31*(3), 225–235. doi:10.1007/s10865-008-9151-x

Luoma, J., Drake, C. E., Kohlenberg, B. S., & Hayes, S. C. (2011). Substance abuse and psychological flexibility: The development of a new measure. *Addiction Research & Theory*, *19*(1), 3–13. doi:10.3109/16066359.2010.524956

MacKenzie, M. B., & Kocovski, N. L. (2010). Self-reported acceptance of social anxiety symptoms: Development and validation of the Social Anxiety–Acceptance and Action Questionnaire. *International Journal of Behavioral Consultation and Therapy*, *6*, 214–232. doi:10.1037/h0100909

MacKenzie, M. B., Kocovski, N. L., Blackie, R. A., Carrique, L. C., Fleming, J. E., & Antony, M. M. (2017). Development of a brief version of the Social Anxiety-Acceptance and Action Questionnaire. *Journal of Psychopathology and Behavioral Assessment*, *39*(2), 342–354. doi:10.1007/s10862-016-9585-3

Martins, M. J. R. V., Castilho, P., Macedo, A. F., Pereira, A. T., Vagos, P., Carvalho, D., . . . Barreto Carvalho, C. (2018). Willingness and Acceptance of Delusions Scale: Early findings on a new instrument for psychological flexibility. *Psychosis*, *10*(3), 198–207. doi:10.1080/17522439.2018.1502340

McCracken, L. M., Vowles, K. E., & Eccleston, C. (2004). Acceptance of chronic pain: Component analysis and a revised assessment method. *Pain*, *107*(1), 159–166. doi:10.1016/j.pain.2003.10.012

Morrison, K. L., Smith, B. M., Ong, C. W., Lee, E. B., Friedel, J. E., Odum, A., . . . Twohig, M. P. (2019). Effects of acceptance and commitment therapy on impulsive decision-making. *Behavior Modification*. doi:10.1177/0145445519833041

Ong, C. W., Lee, E. B., Krafft, J., Terry, C. L., Barrett, T. S., Levin, M. E., & Twohig, M. P. (2019). A randomized controlled trial of acceptance and commitment therapy for clinical perfectionism. *Journal of Obsessive-Compulsive and Related Disorders, 22.* doi:10.1016/j.jocrd.2019.100444

Palmeira, L., Cunha, M., Pinto-Gouveia, J., Carvalho, S., & Lillis, J. (2016). New developments in the assessment of weight-related experiential avoidance (AAQW-Revised). *Journal of Contextual Behavioral Science, 5*(3), 193–200. doi:10.1016/j.jcbs.2016.06.001

Sandoz, E. K., Wilson, K. G., Merwin, R. M., & Kellum, K. K. (2013). Assessment of body image flexibility: The Body Image-Acceptance and Action Questionnaire. *Journal of Contextual Behavioral Science, 2*(1-2), 39–48. doi:10.1016/j.jcbs.2013.03.002

Shawyer, F., Ratcliff, K., Mackinnon, A., Farhall, J., Hayes, S. C., & Copolov, D. (2007). The Voices Acceptance and Action Scale (VAAS): Pilot data. *Journal of Clinical Psychology, 63*(6), 593–606. doi:10.1002/jclp.20366

Spatola, C. A., Cappella, E. A., Goodwin, C. L., Baruffi, M., Malfatto, G., Facchini, M., . . . Molinari, E. (2014). Development and initial validation of the Cardiovascular Disease Acceptance and Action Questionnaire (CVD-AAQ) in an Italian sample of cardiac patients. *Frontiers in Psychology 5,* 1284. doi:10.3389/fpsyg.2014.01284

Westin, V. Z., Hayes, S. C., & Andersson, G. (2008). Is it the sound or your relationship to it? The role of acceptance in predicting tinnitus impact. *Behaviour Research and Therapy, 46*(12), 1259–1265. doi:10.1016/j.brat.2008.08.008

Whiting, D. L., Deane, F. P., Ciarrochi, J., McLeod, H. J., & Simpson, G. K. (2015). Validating measures of psychological flexibility in a population with acquired brain injury. *Psychological Assessment, 27*(2), 415. doi:10.1037/pas0000050

Wicksell, R. K., Lekander, M., Sorjonen, K., & Olsson, G. L. (2010). The Psychological Inflexibility in Pain Scale (PIPS)—Statistical properties and model fit of an instrument to assess change processes in pain related disability. *European Journal of Pain, 14*(7), 771 e771–714. doi:10.1016/j.ejpain.2009.11.015

General Guide to the ACT
Therapeutic Context

Over the past 15 years, I have worked with many professionals who are trying to learn how to do ACT. Graduate students and interns have actually been the easiest to train because they are less set in their worldviews and therapy styles. It can be more difficult to teach more established therapists how to do ACT well. Even though they are fast at picking up techniques, they have a habit of incorporating those skills into their existing worldview and therapy styles. For example, if a client says something like, "Nothing ever seems to work out for me," someone new to ACT might correctly recognize fusion but incorrectly state, "See how you are fusing with that thought right now." In case you are wondering, a better response would be highlighting the function of that thought, with, "And how does that thought affect you?" One could also teach defusing with a statement like, "It is all really in how you respond to that thought." In ACT, a function-based response is needed. This means responding to the function, purpose, or effect of the client's words, rather than their content.

I have also supervised people who started out therapy by explaining the ACT model to the client. They literally drew the hexaflex on a whiteboard and explained what each process was. While they are technically teaching the six ACT processes of change, the manner in which the processes are being taught will render the actual incorporation of those six processes of change unlikely.

The first psychotherapy I (M.P.T.) learned to do was ACT, and I only learned how to do traditional cognitive-behavioral therapy (CBT) on my internship. Frankly, I found that doing traditional CBT was surprisingly difficult; understanding the model and manner in which it is implemented took me several months. Although I quickly learned the techniques and what to say, it took much longer to really get the why and how, knowing what choices to make from this new worldview.

I tell this to illustrate that learning how to do a new treatment like ACT is more than learning techniques or memorizing what to say in each session.

You also need to incorporate the ACT model into your worldview and understand the finer points of how ACT is implemented. This is especially important with ACT, which emphasizes the therapeutic relationship as a vehicle for helping clients become more psychologically flexible. So, really getting the underlying therapeutic stance and bringing that into your interactions with clients is critical.

We (ACT therapists) conceptualize psychological issues that stem from psychological inflexibility as the result of maladaptive side effects of cognition. Through ACT, we try to teach clients to interact with their thoughts and other inner experiences in a new way so that the same verbal stimuli have a different impact on their actions. We believe the therapeutic context is an important medium in which to do that. Therapy is a place where clients can learn to interact with thoughts and feelings differently. Hopefully, the therapeutic relationship and context are strong enough that this new way of interacting with internal experiences transfers to situations outside of therapy. Then, as clients have success with this new way of interacting, they can experience the reinforcers that come along with these actions. These actions will continue because they work for the client in achieving their goals and doing what matters.

In this chapter, we cover key tips on how to make therapy more ACT-consistent. This will include issues related to therapy style, the therapist's orientation toward the work, the way in which therapy is presented, relationship issues, and stylistic aspects. In many ways, these are the hardest to teach in a book. Viewing some videos of ACT might be helpful for learning what ACT feels like. Still, some general guidance will, hopefully, start you down the right path.

ACT BASICS

Acknowledge our shared, common challenges of being human

The issues that clients experience are functionally the same issues just about everyone on the planet experiences, including you. Your clients might experience them more often and more intensely than others, but these struggles are the same at a functional level. Almost everyone experiences fear, frustration, feelings of rejection, and so on. Our clients have generally gotten into a deep and messy struggle with their inner experiences. Presenting inner experiences in this way can be particularly helpful, as it shows clients that nothing is inherently wrong with them. They simply got into an unworkable pattern. We understand their situation because we deal with many of the same things. We also have thoughts we do not like, that show up at the wrong time, and that interfere with the things we want to do. While our inner experiences may get in the way less, we can still relate to clients' issue as fellow humans. *Teach, model, and act like it is OK to have all sorts of inner experiences.*

Accept clients as they are and do not treat them like babies

I (M.P.T.) once had a client tell me she thought about killing herself over the weekend. I believe my response was something like, "How powerful were those thoughts?" and "What did you do with them?" Making a mental note to assess risk later in the session, we continued that discussion, focusing on how she interacted with those thoughts. I treated her suicidal thoughts like other thoughts we had discussed at previous sessions, focusing on the function of the thought (how she reacts to it) rather than its content. I did not make a big deal out of them. Toward the end of the conversation I said something like, "As long as you don't act on those thoughts, we will have time to figure all this out." At the end of our course of therapy I asked her what she learned that made the biggest difference to her. She said, "When I was suicidal, you were so calm and acted like I was fine and all would be OK. That really helped me see my struggles in a different way." I think treating her thoughts as just thoughts helped her to treat her thoughts similarly. I was able to model something she needed to practice. I acted like it was OK to have those thoughts, and so she acted like it was OK to have those thoughts. Although I was sure to assess the severity and risk of suicidality later that session, I didn't start there or treat the thoughts themselves as a sign she was at imminent risk. If I had treated the thought itself as dangerous and scary, then she would have as well, and we would have lost a perfect opportunity to practice defusion together.

Here is another way of looking at this issue. As a therapist I am pretty even-keeled. My mood and demeanor stay pretty constant and I am primarily focused on behavior change. If the client presents with low mood or with lots of energy, I still stay pretty constant. I supervise many students and I find they shift along with the client. I think they are trying to be validating and responsive to the client. There is nothing particularly problematic about that, other than possibly indicating to clients that mood is something worth responding to. What I see that concerns me is when a client shows up with depressed mood and a typically upbeat therapist starts coddling the client. The therapist slows down their speech, gets quiet, and starts speaking in a sensitive way. When watching the video, it feels to me that the client is being protected because they are in a sensitive place. I prefer to model that clients can handle sad emotions and treat them accordingly. For example, I was doing a situational exposure with a client who was somewhat resistant to the exercise, and I gently kept the pressure on because I thought the action the client was attempting to engage in was reasonable for their place in therapy. The fact that I asked like it was totally fine for the client, I think, encouraged the client to engage.

This even-keeled approach is one way of communicating acceptance, but remember, it is the function (impact) you have on the client, not the topography (what it looks like). There are a lot of ways to model acceptance with your clients, and we encourage you to seek out opportunities to see different therapists at work (in videos, trainings, etc.). The important part is to model for clients that whatever thoughts and feelings come up are natural and OK, and that they are not bad, scary, true, or otherwise overpowering experiences that have to be acted on or avoided at all costs. *In summary, model that internal experiences are OK to have. Your client will eventually follow your lead.*

It is always about the client's experience: You learn from doing

As I was providing consultation to my colleague this morning we talked about how to help a client diagnosed with obsessive-compulsive disorder (OCD) see her obsessions differently. The client feared that if she had impure thoughts about a man he would then be more likely to sexually assault her. To those of you familiar with thought–action fusion, you will recognize this response style: Thinking something makes it more likely it will happen. As a bystander, we know our thoughts do not really make events more or less likely—at least in the way we are presenting it here. My consultee and I talked about what experiential activities the client could do to see that thoughts have no effects on the odds of events happening. For example, she could interview her friends or design experiments. Both these examples are consistent with best practice and would likely be helpful. But if we are looking to help the client see this obsession differently, the most powerful way to do so is through real-life experiences. We would want her to have many direct experiences that would help her see these obsessions differently. Thus, we talked about setting up as many situations as possible that would bring up her obsessions so that she could practice interacting with them differently.

We do everything we can to work with experiences in vivo rather than discuss them. We certainly avoid telling a client how something works. We would rather give them the space to work with it and then help them accurately appreciate what just occurred (i.e., see contingencies as they are, rather than the verbal representation of them). *The client's life will show the client how things work. Create experiences in and outside of session that teach psychological flexibility.*

Metaphorical and experiential

As written earlier, we do everything we can to make therapy experiential; the title of the first book on ACT was *Acceptance and Commitment Therapy: An Experiential Approach to Therapy* (Hayes, Strosahl, & Wilson, 1999). The main idea is that people will rigidly follow rules. At worst, rules are inaccurate; at best, they are generally accurate. However, for most rules, there are times when they do not apply. For example, a rule like "be nice to others" is usually true, but there are times when being kind to others could lead to being taken advantage of. We believe rules naturally developed through interactions with the world are more flexible to the contingencies that are present. Thus, therapy is delivered via experiences—rather than didactic explanations—as much as possible.

The number one option for ACT, if possible, is to teach these concepts in an actual situation. If the client struggles with anxiety, find situations that elicit anxiety and then teach psychological flexibility. If the client struggles with depression, work with depression that is present in the moment.

Therapy can be relatively easy if you follow these steps: (1) ask the client about a struggle they had since you last saw them; (2) continue to ask about that event using open-ended questions; (3) once the target internal experience, such as thoughts, feelings, sensations, or urges, starts to show, keep pushing; and (4) when you feel there is enough internal experience present to work with, start coaching the client on how to use psychological flexibility with that experience.

Here is a simplified example of the general pattern we suggest for your average ACT session.

THERAPIST (T): Tell me about a moment this week when you felt triggered.

CLIENT (C): I was at work and my supervisor asked me to go clean the back of the store.

T: What happened for you in that moment?

C: I had a reaction like, "What the hell. That's the worst job. I've been here a long time. Give that job to a new person. I bet he's giving it to me out of spite."

T: What else were you thinking?

C: I just thought this was BS. Nobody wants to clean up the mess in the back of the store. It's the worst.

T: Which emotions where you experiencing at that time?

C: Anger. Hopelessness. Frustration.

T: Are you experiencing any of the same thoughts and emotions now, as we talk about it?

C: Yes. I'm sort of worked up.

T: OK. Are you willing to practice something with me right now?

C. Sure.

T: Tell me how negatively you experience the feeling you are experiencing right now.

C: I hate it. I feel weak and helpless.

T: Thanks. Rather than running from this, trying to lessen it, or otherwise make it different, let's just hang out in it. But let's not just suffer through it. Let's find a reason that it is worth hanging out in. Tell me a way life would be a little better if this did not push you around.

C: I would stay out of trouble at work. There have certainly been times when I've blown my top and gotten into trouble at work.

T: OK, cool. Let's go a step further than staying out of trouble and go toward a job that you find meaningful. Let's picture you heading off on a journey with a destination of "meaningful work" and in your backpack are thoughts like "I hate this guy" or "Life is unfair." There are also feelings like anger, frustration, helplessness, and so on. It's just that you have to bring this backpack along with you. Setting it down is not an option; everything you need is in there, like your food, water, and rain gear. If you want to bring the stuff you need to live, you also have to bring along some stuff you don't like.

The target emotion was a little bit present, so we asked open-ended questions to make it more present. Once it was notably there, we moved into skills teaching, which can be done through experiential exercises or metaphors. Although this example was brief and contrived, it illustrated our point that ACT is best done experientially. *Find or create experiences to teach psychological flexibility experientially.*

Resist the urge to explain what the metaphor means at the end

Humans dislike uncertainty or confusion, and it is pretty common for the therapist to feel the urge to make sure the client understands what the therapist just taught, even though clarifying things may not always be therapeutically indicated. For example, saying "Struggling with anxiety is like struggling with quicksand" is more effective than saying "Struggling with anxiety is like struggling with quicksand—you know, the more you fight against it the larger it will be." This is because by stating the rule, you are undermining their opportunity to contact direct contingencies in their life, to explore and reflect on their own experiences with anxiety, and to learn the consequences of how they react to it. You might as well just tell the client to not struggle against their anxiety. Instead, try and engage the client throughout every exercise and metaphor so you can track whether they are following or getting anything from it. For instance, if we were to expand on the backpack exercise from the previous section it might look like this:

T: I'd like to do a little exercise with you. Are you OK with that?

C: Yes.

T: OK, let's say you are going on a journey. It's a long one, maybe a couple weeks. But because this is therapy we are not talking about a trip to Hawaii or a national park but a journey toward something important to you. Like most things that are important, you can only work toward it; it is very hard to accomplish. For the sake of this exercise, what journey do you want to talk about?

C: I hate my job and want a different one.

T: I am totally cool with helping you go after something else, but I would like that to be motivated by going after something better, rather than running from something frustrating. What is it?

C: It's lots of things, but a part of it is I stay where I am because it is easy, but I have no passion for retail. I'm in school to work with animals, but there are very few jobs in that area and retail is everywhere.

T: OK, let's focus on going toward what you care about rather than away from what annoys you. So, we are going on a journey to work with animals. That is your direction. But to go on this journey you will need a backpack for food, water, appropriate clothing, and so on. Tell me what you would pack.

C: Yeah, water, food, rain gear, maps, sunscreen, and stuff like that. I hike so I get it.

T: But you also have to carry along some things that are just going to show up. Fear, frustration, anxiety, and anger also get thrown in the backpack. Tell me about those things.

C: Oh, you know, I get pissed off, I hate things, I get frustrated. It's how I am.

T: Tell me more.

C: When things don't go my way, my emotions build up. I struggle to listen to others and be told what to do. I hate doing things that feel beneath me.

T: How will this show up on this journey?

C: I'm sure it will not be easy. I will likely have to interact with others. Lots of stuff.

T: OK, cool. All these things as well as the gear you need are in your backpack. Are you cool with carrying all this along?

C: Do I have a choice?

T: You do. You can have this pack strapped on tight while focusing on moving forward. You can also keep checking in the pack to see what is in there: complaining about how much there is, going over in your mind about how unfair it is that your pack is so heavy. You can compare your pack to others' packs. So I'll ask again: Are you willing to carry the pack just as it is?

C: Wow. Good question.

Keep teaching through metaphor. Do not summarize into a rule.

Fit of example/metaphor is more important than saying it correctly

Treatment matching is important. Using the example of tolerating the distress of waiting for your table to be ready at a fine restaurant probably will not resonate with a rural rancher as might the frustration of a long and drawn-out repair project. We will not belabor this point, but as you work with your client, try and match your examples to the client's life. If you are going to use a sport example, ask what sport they are into. If they are not into any sport, ask them what they are into. We would assume most things in life have a similar growth curve, from being difficult and frustrating to being easier but still a struggle at times.

Descriptions that match with the client will have a greater impact and be more memorable. For example, all of us authors enjoy rock climbing. A discussion involving climbing will be much more relatable and impactful than one about tennis, which we are not really into. It is fine if you do not know the intricacies of your client's interest; they can explain that to you. Trying to match your discussions to things that matter to your client will be more therapeutically meaningful and show that you are individualizing treatment to your client. Here is a quick hypothetical example:

T: I'd like to share an example of how we show willingness with everyday events. What is a sport you are into—tennis, basketball, football?

C: I really don't do those types of sports. I'm into rock climbing.

T: Cool. I don't know much about that but I'd be shocked if learning to rock climb was notably different from learning other sports. Tell me about your goals with climbing when you first started.

C: I was just doing it with friends for fun, but pretty quickly I wanted to be decent at it and do harder climbs.

T: OK, tell me about the emotions you experienced as you were learning.

C: It went back and forth between enjoyment and frustration. I had good times and then would really struggle with some of the new things I was learning. I'd struggle and then slowly get better at them.

T: Do you feel you have come a long way in your climbing?

C: Yes, but I also have a very long way to go. It's weird.

T: How is this like our work with your phobia?

C: Very, very similar.

T: How is it different?

C: Good question. I think I gave myself a lot more space with learning to climb than I do in therapy. I never thought I'd be a hotshot climber in a few months, but I want to be over my phobia ASAP. That's sort of weird.

We hope you, the reader, can see how matching the description to the client can help keep the client engaged and interested in therapy. The therapist knew little about climbing but was open to letting the client describe the sport. If we were the therapist, we would read a little about climbing so we had some examples to share with the client at future sessions. It would keep the client's interest and build rapport. For example:

T: After our session, I started looking up climbing on the internet and saw that two climbers had just set the speed record for climbing the nose on El Capitan. How much work would it take for you to get to that place and what would you have to do to get there? Now, I kind of doubt you could set a new speed record, but is that a climb you could accomplish?

C: I guess technically, but there are many climbing and equipment techniques I would need to learn. I would need to be in much better shape. I'd have to practice a lot. So maybe, but it would be a ton of work.

T: And it seems you could break the work down into pieces and work on them individually. How is that like our work?

c: I guess you can work toward any life goal. You would just take it piece by piece. You might get there or you might not, but you can try.

Use examples and metaphors that are meaningful to the client.

ACT IS A PROCESS-BASED INTERVENTION

The client's experiences are right—no arguing

ACT focuses on function over form. Whether something is technically right or wrong is secondary to its effect on the client. Thus, watch for the pull to argue when the client says something that is factually wrong. Focus on what effect the thought has on the client. For example, if a client says, "I feel like I am going to pass out when I am experiencing a panic attack," rather than discussing how passing out is very unlikely to occur because blood pressure is elevated during a panic attack, ask how that fear affects the client and what they do when it shows up. Similarly, if you are working with a client diagnosed with OCD and they say, "I tried the acceptance things you talked about and I had the worst week ever," do not tell them "acceptance is a skill and you need to practice" or "maybe you were doing it wrong." Just listen. There is something accurate in the client's experience. It is your job to help the client find that and use it to guide their future choices. Sometimes, they report things that are not accurate, but give them time to contact more experiences and they will see how things work for them. *Let clients' real experiences guide their choices.*

Don't explain the six processes or draw the hexaflex

This is one of the most common "mistakes" I see new ACT therapists commit. In many other therapies, conceptualizing the case and the process through which treatment works is a common way to start therapy. But if you understand the downfall of rule governance and psychological inflexibility, you can probably see the downside of teaching clients a model of how psychopathology develops and how to get out of it. In ACT, we prefer to help clients pay closer attention to how things are working for them. Our goal is to decrease rule following. If clients can pay closer attention to how things work in their lives, then they can figure out ways of responding that will work better in the long run. You will need to notice your pull to explain things. Walk the client through ACT; do not teach them about ACT. I often think about it like a magic show (not that ACT is magic) in which being walked through the trick is what makes it fascinating. If you were told what is occurring or where you need to be watching, it would take much of the enjoyment out of it. Another way I like to explain it to my practicum students is, *help the client figure it out on their own.* I had a practicum student say, "It's one point if you say it and two points if the client says it first."

The importance of modeling psychological flexibility

Therapy might be the only setting in the client's life where psychological flexibility is normal. You generally have about 1 hour a week to help the client see the benefits of responding to internal experiences in this new way. It is hard to have a lot of impact when the rest of the world is telling the client to feel differently, that having only positive emotions is the best way to do things, and that one should not experience *negative* emotions. I remember my first training in ACT and was honestly shocked to see the world presented this way. It was the opposite from everything I had learned thus far.

As we mentioned previously, this is key when working with painful and scary inner experiences. There are key opportunities in therapy where you can practice the same ACT skills you are teaching your clients, modeling how to do this work in the moment. As therapists we all have things that clients can say or do that "hook" us, where we start responding inflexibly to the content of what is being said, rather than focusing on the function and our treatment plan. For example, each of us authors have had clients engage in an extended speech on political issues that vary from our own beliefs. In our best moments as therapists we catch our natural, inflexible reactions (to argue, to check out, or to wait for the rant to stop) and instead reorient to the function (what is going on for the client, how does this link to what we are working on, and what might I do to model and elicit psychological flexibility). For example, we might shift a frustrated, fused rant about politics by acknowledging the emotions and thoughts that are present, reflecting how we notice our own minds getting caught up and fused with what is right and wrong, and shifting to notice the process of our mind "doing its thing" while considering what we want to focus on doing with the time we have.

The therapist has a lot of credibility, so what you say and how you act stands out to the client. *Therefore, you need to be present and prepared to notice when you get caught up in psychological inflexibility and to shift to model psychological flexibility throughout the session.*

DISCLOSURE

Disclosure is an excellent way to teach and model psychological flexibility. I use disclosure in almost every session. It is a great way to show that every verbal human struggles with similar internal experiences; it is just that some of us have more practice and skill responding to them in effective ways. It can be really useful for a client to see that the therapist also experiences anxiety, depression, and uncertainty. We might even not like experiencing those internal experiences. Disclosure is also a valuable way to model flexibility for your clients, describing what is coming up for you in the moment and how you are responding flexibly.

Some of my practicum students struggle with disclosure, and I can see why. Disclosure can sound like you are supposed to put out your dark secrets. I do not think that is accurate. You need to be professional and ethical. If disclosures are in the client's best interest and are appropriate, they can be useful. Remember that, like everything you do in therapy, the focus should be on the function you want to have with clients, doing things that help your client become more psychologically flexible, in line with the case conceptualization and treatment goals. As it is hard to provide rules on what level of disclosure is appropriate, we will offer a few examples of generally appropriate levels of sharing.

> T: I often feel quite frustrated when doing homework with my children. It bothers me, as I wish I enjoyed the time with them but that is just not how I feel.

> T: As a professor I have lots of opportunities to lecture. I have different levels of anxiety when lecturing. Sometimes it's a 0 out of 10, and in the past few years I have had some 9s out of 10. The thing that has surprised me is the higher levels of anxiety are not all that predictable. I've spoken to hundreds of people and had low anxiety, and I've spoken to 20 but a look someone gave me set me off. It's odd how anxiety works.

> T: In my life there are emotions I have learned I should usually listen to and emotions I usually don't listen to. For example, if I see my wife and feel love toward her I'll usually say something. Nothing huge, but I'll tell her I love her, or I appreciate her. She always likes that. But when I am feeling frustrated toward her, I have learned that in our relationship, that is not the right time to say it. We do better discussing it later in the day, when we are feeling less frustrated.

I hope you see that all three of these examples are pretty harmless; raising children can feel frustrating, I experience anxiety at times when lecturing, and I feel love for and frustration with my wife. I am pretty confident these emotions apply to just about everyone on the planet. But putting them out there creates a context in which we can discuss functional ways to respond to them.

We also encourage you to take opportunities to be appropriately bold in your disclosures with clients. By *bold* we mean taking a measured risk to put out there with your client a reaction you are having in the moment. By *appropriate* we mean doing so in a way that is likely to have the function you want with your client, based on the case conceptualization and treatment goals. When you notice yourself having a strong internal reaction to your client or an urge to respond inflexibly (to over-explain, avoid a topic, argue), consider if it is an opportunity to model and elicit psychological flexibility. One pattern we use is to state a thought or feeling we are having in response to a client in a defused, accepting way; call out the pull to respond inflexibly and the costs of that response; and orient ourselves toward a flexible response instead.

> T: I'm noticing right now that I have the urge to "save you" from this feeling of anxiety. I want to reassure you that it's going to be OK. And my mind is telling me to "come up with a solution, quick." But that would be doing

more of the same in a way, and the things you have been saying don't work and make you feel stuck. And I'm here to help you do something different in your life. What if instead we just watched this anxiety and the urge to make it go away? Just noticing it for what it is while we continue the session.

These types of disclosures can feel bold, and this boldness can help break an inflexible pattern for yourself or your client. *Small, safe disclosures can be useful; look for opportunities to be appropriately bold in your disclosures to model flexibility.*

Tip on how to remember what to go over in session

Please do not take this as a rule, but generally, when doing ACT, we do not have a clipboard or notes on our laps. Maybe it is just tradition or weird rule-following, but having a clipboard feels like there is something between the client and the therapist. It sort of establishes that you, as the therapist, are in charge. It feels like good modeling to sit there equally, with no materials between you and the client.

But I can see you asking, "How am I supposed to remember what to do?" I was here once too, and I found that a bulleted list on a small sheet of paper was enough to keep me on track. I would basically have a list of 5–10 words that reminded me of where I was planning on going in the session. For example, you might have one that looks like this:

- Check-in (homework)
- Willingness
- Two scales
- Little defusion
- Touch on values
- Behavioral commitment
- Homework sheet

If you need to remember what to do in a session, make a short list of bullet points and set it on the table next to you.

Little language issues

As you get more talented in ACT you will find there are a handful of language conventions that are common in lay language that support psychological inflexibility. Because this is an introductory book, we will only present two of them, but as you get more into this therapy, I am sure you will run into many more. Some of these will sound awkward the first time you say them and they might not work well in lay speech, but they can be helpful in teaching psychological flexibility.

CLIENT EXPERIENCES VERSUS IS AN EMOTION

People often say, "I'm depressed," or "I'm anxious," or "I'm mad." It is less common to say one feels that way. But it makes a difference. If one *is* something then it is really difficult to change that. If one is tall, or skinny, or from Wisconsin, then those are generally stable. This is in contrast to something that changes from hour to hour or day to day, like our inner experiences. I would never say I am anxious in the same way that I am tall. But most people talk that way, and it gives the experience of anxious permanence and power. Therefore, we prefer to say *experiencing* anxiety, *feeling* sad, or *noticing* depressive thoughts. All these ways of talking about inner experiences present them as events that the person observes instead of is defined by. *Talk about inner experiences as transitory rather than stable.*

INNER EXPERIENCES ARE DESCRIBED OBJECTIVELY (E.G., big or small), not subjectively (e.g., good or bad)

Just like the previous example, it is easy to fall into calling emotions *good* or *bad*, even when we all know we do not really mean it that way. But these little slips reinforce the notion that certain inner experiences are OK to have and others are not. This is all conceptually pretty straightforward when we are talking about anxiety, depression, or pain. We all know that life without these inner experiences would not be functional. We suggest calling the internal experiences what they are without the descriptors. The same goes for happiness, love, and other so-called positive emotions—just call them by name rather than calling them *good* emotions.

There are more complicated inner experiences, such as trauma memories, panic attacks, gruesome obsessions, or chronic pain. These are inner experiences that almost everyone would agree are disturbing, gross, or otherwise aversive. Even then, it is important to use language that sounds more objective to describe them. You might say, "thoughts that are more of a struggle for you," or "thoughts that go against who you are." "Painful" seems like an OK way to describe a memory of a trauma, but "bad" does not sound so good. You can even be straightforward with the client about the situation:

T: How are you doing with the obsessions?

c: I can let them be there sometimes, and other times they overwhelm me— they are just so disturbing.

T: Yes, I can understand. A thought about harming a loved one can really grab you. Let's make sure we are able to tell the difference between a thought about harming a loved one and actually doing it. The act would be disturbing, but what do you make of a thought about it?

Describe inner experiences as objectively as possible.

BUILDING YOUR COMPETENCE WITH ACT

This way of doing therapy can feel like a lot to absorb for those who are new to ACT. The principles discussed here might fit broadly with your own views on mental health and therapy, but they might also leave you unclear as to how to actually do this with clients and bring all of these principles to bear in the moment. This is exactly why we wrote this book. The rest of this book will walk you through a session-by-session protocol on how to actually go through a course of ACT with a client. It takes time to learn how to embody these key ACT principles, and the best way to learn is by doing it. We recommend reviewing this chapter a few times as you continue working with clients. As you work with your clients, keep these core principles in the back of your mind, looking for opportunities to practice ACT as a way of doing therapy, rather than as just a set of techniques.

REFERENCE

Hayes, S. C., Strosahl, K., & Wilson, K. G. (1999). *Acceptance and commitment therapy: An experiential approach to behavior change*. New York: Guilford Press.

Session 1

ACT Orientation and Creative Hopelessness

This session has two phases: (1) help the client orient to what occurs in therapy in general and ACT specifically, and (2) implement the phase of ACT called *creative hopelessness*. The overarching aim of the session is to have the client start to interact with their thoughts, feelings, and bodily sensations in a different way and to start making choices based on what they care about rather than what they are feeling. We need to set a new stage for therapy and life in order to do this. In particular, we believe establishing a strong foundation with creative hopelessness and control as the problem (covered in Chapter 5) can make work later on in therapy go a lot more smoothly.

Although this typically takes us a session, feel free to spend a couple sessions with your client on this chapter, depending on how quickly they grasp these new ideas. The same guideline is true for the chapters that follow. The session timeline we outline is just a guide, and your clients may require more or less time. We recommend meeting your clients where they are at instead of trying to rush through the content of these chapters. The findings from the ACT ADVISOR (Figure 2.2) will help guide you as you work through this chapter and the later ones.

SETTING THE STAGE FOR THERAPY

1. Ask the client what they want from therapy

This is a relatively straightforward question that is often missed in therapy: "Why are you here?" or "What do you want to get out of therapy?" Most professionals know that the goal of therapy is to help clients live healthier and more meaningful lives. Sometimes we equate that to being happy or free from certain "negative" inner experiences, but if we think about it, we would say emotional regulation is merely a means toward living a more meaningful life. Clients are less familiar with this way of thinking. Clients, like all people, make up rules about ways to fix things. Just like we have rules, clients will usually have some sort of rule that, once certain inner experiences are reasonably controlled, life will be better. This is a rule that is very difficult to follow and is really more like a rigged game. ACT takes the stance—supported by data—that inner experiences are difficult to meaningfully control and that attempts to do so often cause more harm than good. Still, clients will usually report they are in therapy to feel less depressed or anxious, to be happy, or to feel good about themselves.

We need to help them look at this situation differently, by asking them, "What will change in your life if you lessen that inner experience?" You want to know what the client wants to be different in their life. Typical answers will be that they will be happier, enjoy life more, and do things that have been difficult, such as being more engaged with work, friends, and other meaningful activities. Now is not the time to challenge the conceptualization that changing inner experience is the key to changing the way one lives, but to gently suggest there are other ways to think about it. In addition, you will establish that focusing on how one is living is an important metric for a "good life." The hope is to get the client somewhat ready to start thinking about their situation a little differently. The following steps will also help with that.

2. Ask the client about their understanding of therapy: Get on the same page

You are trying to learn the client's rules about therapy while simultaneously teaching the client to hold these rules flexibly because they may not be accurate. As described in the Chapter 1 of this book, a general goal of ACT is to vary (e.g., make it happen at some times but not at other times) the influence of language on the actions of the client. Most clients have some level of knowledge of therapy. Sometimes this knowledge will be really helpful to therapy and other times it will not be. For example, if a client has a history with a compassionate and cooperative therapist, there will likely be an expectation of that again. Whereas if the last therapist gave a lot of instruction and taught skills counter to ACT, there will be expectations for similar therapy. There are even times when the client has no therapy experience, and maybe what they know about it is from television. These are the most interesting clients to ask, "What do you foresee happening in therapy?" We have heard clients say things like, "Well I pictured myself lying down, with you sitting behind me, and me talking about myself." The following is an example of how such a conversation might go:

THERAPIST (T): Please tell me what you think is going to happen in therapy.
CLIENT (C): I don't really understand the question.
T: Each client has their own history with therapy or their own expectations of what therapy will be like. I'd like to know what you think we are going to work on together and what you expect from therapy.

c: OK. I have been in therapy before and we worked on decreasing my depression. I found therapy to be helpful. My therapist generally helped me see how I think about life as well as how I think about myself.

t: This is really useful. What is your goal in therapy?

c: To be less depressed.

t: What do you think of that goal?

c: Sounds good to me (laughs).

t: OK. And what do you think things will be like between you and me?

c: That's an interesting question. I generally don't think about that. I guess I just figure that you are in charge and you're going to teach me what to do.

t: Thank you for sharing this information. I've found it really helpful. We have a long road ahead of us and rather than mapping it all out before we get started, I'd rather just tell you some basic things about how I do therapy. First, while I do know a good amount about psychology, I see us both as experts. You are an expert on how things work for you. But a funny thing can happen in life: we can go about our days and there are many things to learn, but we don't see them. I have a sense of things people miss or misinterpret. All I am going to do in therapy is help you see some things that are already there but you are missing and offer you some new options you can try out and see how they work for you.

3. Discuss what a "good" outcome is

The goal of this phase is to begin undermining the rule that the only "good" outcome is less of a specific internal experience while offering the alternative rule that "quality of life" might also be a good goal for therapy. Clients generally enter therapy with the hope that the therapist can decrease whatever internal experience (e.g., anxiety, depression) is unpleasant for the client. This expectation is likely based on rules clients hold. The first rule is that certain internal experiences are bad. This is a rule that is almost unwritten in Western culture. However, most people would agree that no internal experience is inherently problematic. Inner experiences are only problems if they negatively affect people. The second rule many clients have is that they can start working on quality of life once certain internal events are lessened. Even though anxiety and depression cannot actually stop people from engaging in certain activities, clients follow rules that say just that.

An ACT therapist generally does not directly challenge a rule, because that would be replacing a rule the client did not learn via experience with another one learned through society. We aim to create a space in which the client can learn to hold rules flexibly and develop more functional ones based on their lives. Thus, you need to have a conversation about whether thoughts, feelings, and emotions are actually bad and whether they need to change.

T: What one thing about you needs to be different to make your life better?

C: I guess I need to handle my depression better. I need to know how to control it better.

T: Why do you want to control your depression?

C: That is easy. If I did not feel this way so often I'd be able to live the way I want, and be the type of person I want to be.

T: How hard is it to do what you want or need to do while feeling this way?

C: It's very hard. It is hard to just feel this way but it's especially hard to do things while feeling this way.

T: If depression was gone, would life be easy?

C: Yes.

T: The first thing I would like you to do is recognize the feelings you are having right now. That feeling of frustration and being overwhelmed tells you something about your situation. Ask yourself: Have you been working hard? And is it getting you to where you want to be? If the answer is "no," then maybe you are playing by unfair rules. Maybe the rule that certain thoughts and feelings are inherently bad is wrong. People seek out fear in movies, rides, and sports but despise fear when it is from a trauma. The rule that you can do what you want in life once the feeling is lessened may also be an inaccurate one. If you ever watch a play or a musical, I bet you are seeing a whole bunch of people who feel quite nervous or anxious *and* they perform quite well.

C: That seems like a lot. That seems really different.

T: I won't tell you what to do. Instead, I will ask you to look at your experience and see what works well and what does not. If you notice things are not working well, I can offer you other options. Tell me, how well are you doing at controlling your depression?

C: Poorly.

T: Is that because you have not tried hard enough to control it?

C: I've tried really hard, actually.

T: Be honest. Has life improved or worsened as you have worked at this?

C: Honestly, things have been going downhill for a while.

T: OK. So maybe the rule about regulating depression is wrong in some ways. Maybe you don't have to control depression better to live a higher-quality life, and we may need to rethink our rules about how you work.

C: OK.

T: But there is an important part here. This means our goals in therapy might be more about how well you can handle your depression rather than how much depression you feel. This makes a difference. When I ask you, "How was your week?" I am asking, "What did you do? What percent of the time did you do things you wanted to do? How much did you let depression push you around?" I am not asking, "How much depression did you feel?"

C: Are you saying how much depression I feel does not matter?

T: It matters in a different way. It matters in the sense that it tells us how hard you had to try or how much effort you had to put in to live the way you want. It's like driving to work on a sunny day or on a stormy day. We might be interested in how long it takes you, but we would understand that the drive on the stormy day will be more difficult and slower.

4. Improvement will not be linear

The goal is to challenge the rule that the client's unwanted inner experience will slowly decrease throughout therapy. As with previous conversations, we are evaluating the utility of rules that are likely unworkable. The first unworkable rule is that the inner experience can easily be changed. Hopefully, that rule got addressed a little in the last conversation. The second unworkable rule is that gains are gradual and linear. People have experiences in life where they get out what they put in. For example, if you work in your garden you can reasonably expect that it will slowly look better. Moreover, if you work all day it will look better than if you work for a few hours. Events occur that are outside of our control. Maybe the gardener will have a beautiful summer, or maybe rain will be scarce.

Our fear as therapists is that if the gains are more "up and down," this pattern will go against the client's rule of what "good therapy" looks like. If it is viewed as "not working" because changes are nonlinear, then there is a greater chance of client dropout. We want the client to enter therapy with the rule that "gains will be nonlinear" and "gains will be measured in terms of quality of life rather than internal experiences." This description is integrated with the next section.

5. Give therapy time to show it is helpful

This "new" approach to therapy will be confusing and even frustrating, change will be slow, and positive change will be in quality of life rather than in emotions, thoughts, or memories. Thus, it is wise to discuss giving therapy a reasonable amount of time to show its utility. We typically explain these issues to clients and ask them how long they think is reasonable to "give ACT a fair shot." Sometimes an analogy is useful, such as, "If you were to take up a new hobby, how much time would you need to spend on it to know if you like it or not?" You can even ask the client about learning new things and what that process is like. For example, you might say, "There is something fun about hiking somewhere new, but I will certainly be more prepared in terms of how much food and water to bring, how sunny the trail is, what shoes are best, and how long it takes the second time I do the hike. I may not even enjoy it that much the first time and have more fun the second time. Some things take time and practice to really appreciate."

Specifically ask the client this: "How many sessions do you think is fair to get a sense of whether this therapy is useful or not? I'm asking you to give me a handful of sessions so we don't judge this impulsively. Just like I noted before, this process will have ups and downs, and two sessions is not enough to get a sense of whether this is helpful or not." Any number in the four or greater range is good. That can be presented as about a month to try this new therapy.

HELPING THE CLIENT SEE THAT CONTROLLING INNER EXPERIENCES BACKFIRES: CREATIVE HOPELESSNESS

Creative hopelessness is an odd term for a phase of therapy. To give some historical background, creative hopelessness was a term for the initial phase of ACT when it was first developed. At that time, ACT already had a strong focus on processes of change but was still adherent to some therapeutic procedures. Creative hopelessness was one of the original procedures everyone learning ACT knew how to do. If you purchase the original ACT book (Hayes, Strosahl, & Wilson, 1999), you will see that Chapter 4 is on creative hopelessness. Creative hopelessness is covered in books less so now than when ACT first started because we think it is more important to understand the six ACT processes of change than to master specific techniques. We still think that is the case, but, as written earlier, learning how to flexibly apply these six techniques can be too hard a hurdle for some to overcome. We find creative hopelessness is a nice way to get rolling with a client. In our experience, it goes smoothly a high percentage of the time.

The goal of creative hopelessness is to help the client see the *hopelessness* of regulating inner experiences and at the same time intuit a *creative* solution to their problem by being open to a new way of approaching it. To be straightforward, you are guiding clients to contact their lived experiences that will typically tell them the following: (1) inner events are difficult to control in a meaningful way, (2) attempts at regulating the inner experience might be more problematic than having the feeling itself, and (3) the only way out of this situation might be to sidestep the whole thing—to take a completely different approach to the problem: acceptance.

We have developed a way to teach this phase that is simple and generally works. Part of the reason it seems to work is that we know the client has not been able to control their inner experience and that attempts to do so impact quality of life. We know this because the client is seeking therapy. If the client were able to meaningfully change their inner experience, then there probably would not be an issue on which to work. If they were already practicing acceptance, then the inner experience would also not be a clinical issue.

We are not sure how to emphasize the importance of this next statement other than to write it this way: **This is really important. You must figure out what the inner experience is that the client is struggling with!** ACT makes a lot of sense for you and the client if you know the internal experience that the client is struggling with. For example, it may be anxiety in anxiety disorders, depression in mood disorders, urges to use a substance in substance use disorders, pain in pain disorders, urges to pull hair in trichotillomania, and so on. Remember, a core concept in ACT is that people spend a lot of time and energy attempting to control particular inner experiences and not only do these attempts not work, they come at a cost in terms of quality of life. In this exercise, you will walk the client through all the ways in which they have tried to control their inner experiences, see the effects of those attempts, and question whether this overall way of dealing with the inner experience is wise.

The outline of the creative hopelessness exercise is as follows:

- Find the target inner experience.
- How long has the client struggled with this inner experience?
- What has the client done to control this inner experience?
- How well can it be controlled in the short term?
- How well can it be controlled in the long term?
- How is this really working for the client, based on their lived experience?

Find the target inner experience.

Did we mention that it is crucial you determine what the target inner experience is? This whole exercise rests on your knowing that. For every person for whom psychological inflexibility is an issue, there is at least one inner experience that is problematic for them. Figure out what that is and find a term you can use to talk about it. When working with anxiety, it will be *anxiety, fear, obsession*, or some related term. When working with substance use or trichotillomania, it will be *urge*. Finding a term your clients can relate to will help them engage meaningfully in the exercise. You might ask, "What is the thought, feeling, or sensation you struggle with?" (We are going to use anxiety as an example in this section.) Once you nail down a term you can use throughout therapy with the client, write on the whiteboard or a sheet of paper, "Can you control anxiety?"

How long has your client struggled?

Ask, "How long have you struggled with this feeling?" Depending on the age of the client, we might ask whether they struggled with this in grade school, high school, college, in their 30s or 40s, and so on. The goal is to help the client see that this is an old struggle. You might even ask them to think of all the ways this struggle has shown up throughout their life. For example, the client might have been nervous about social things in school, getting a job in college, relationships after that, and now their career. Help your client grasp that this is a timeless struggle that has likely shown up in various permutations.

What has your client done to control this inner experience?

Next say, "I think it is important we get a sense of how anxiety works and how much it is really under your control." You can add, "I would like to let your experience teach us about how these things work." Then, get a list of the ways your client has tried to regulate, minimize, or otherwise escape or avoid anxiety (see Box 4.1 for examples). You will notice there are overt avoidance behaviors, little things people do in their heads, unhealthy moves like using substances, and even healthy activities like yoga, exercise, and praying. While we have provided a list of such behaviors in Box 4.1 as an example, it is important to avoid labeling these things as "good" or "bad" with your client because we are more curious about whether your client can successfully control anxiety. Be sure to get an exhaustive list so the client properly appreciates all their attempts to control inner experiences.

How well does it work to control the inner experience?

Once that list is up, we will usually ask, "So what do you think?" We usually get responses that the list is long or that a lot of time and energy go into those

Box 4.1 EXAMPLE OF LIST OF CONTROL STRATEGIES
IN CREATIVE HOPELESS EXERCISE

Control Strategies
Tell myself "It's OK" [s]
Watch Netflix [s]
Talk to friends [s]
Do yoga [s]
Work out [s]
Drink alcohol [s]
Pray [s]
Take a deep breath [s]
Listen to music [s]
Go for a run [s]
Cry [s]
Vent [s]
Read a book [s]
Use Reddit [s]
Read Buzzfeed lists [s]
Use social media [s]
Isolating self [s]
Procrastinate [s]

s, short term.

strategies. Sometimes the client will wonder what they have missed or not tried yet. Regardless, at this point, say, "This is a nice list. It looks a lot like other ones I have seen. You have tried logical things. I only see reasonable moves up here." Tell the client you are curious how effective these moves are at regulating anxiety. It is important that you indicate you are curious about how well these moves have worked to control the inner experience. We are not asking if they are good life moves. That is not the point of this exercise. After all, healthy moves may not always help to control emotion.

Short-term effectiveness

Tell the client you first want to look at whether these emotion-control strategies are useful in the short term for regulating anxiety (or other inner experiences). *Short-term* refers to a couple minutes or an hour or two. Remind the client that many strategies work in the short term but their effects do not last. For example, I might distract myself while at the dentist to ignore the discomfort of having my teeth scraped. That is a short-term solution because I need to avoid anxiety the next time I go. The move only worked in that moment. We will walk through each move and decide whether the move gets rid of the anxiety in the short term or if it gets rid of it for a long while. Do not focus on whether the move is a good idea. Many control strategies can be healthy things, like yoga or running, but are not effective long-term solutions for regulating inner experience.

We often go through the list and add a little *s* after those that only work in the short term. It usually ends up being most of the items on the list. Sometimes a client will argue that one strategy works really well, is easy to do, or lasts a long time. When that occurs we just agree and say, "Great, we are just looking at the success of your strategies. Sounds good that you have one that works pretty well for you." But usually after going through all the strategies we will find all the moves work fairly well in the short term but not longer than that.

Long-term effectiveness

Next, we say, "What we are really looking for are strategies that work for extended periods of time. If you were to have a plumber fix a leaking pipe in your home, how long would you like that repair to last?" Most of the time the answer is something like, "For the life of the home." Then, we go through the list of strategies and ask what has worked in the long run, by which we mean months or years. This is obviously a bit of a trick question because nothing on the list will have worked that long. If something had worked for that duration, the person would not be seeking therapy. After you have gone through all the strategies and determined none of them has worked in the long term, ask one final question.

How is this really working for you?

After creating this list, most clients feel some frustration or hopelessness. They see a lot of work has gone into solving a problem without real success. It is kind to tell the client that their attempts are reasonable and that they simply did what most people do: They saw a problem and tried to fix it. Whereas this problem-solving approach works for many things outside our skin (e.g., flat tire, lost car keys), struggles under our skin (e.g., anxiety, depression, self-critical thoughts) seem to work differently, so it is hard to find a clear path out of them. At the same time, it is important to get a sense of how this is working for the client based on their real experiences. Specifically, ask:

1. Is the inner experience getting easier or harder to deal with?
2. Are any of these strategies negatively affecting your life?
3. How long can you maintain this fight against your anxiety?

Usually clients report, over time, the inner experience has become a larger issue in their lives. In fact, the more time they spend trying to fix it, the bigger it gets. When going over how these strategies negatively affect their lives, there will usually be a few that cause problems. Clients spend a lot of time attempting to control inner experience, and these attempts detract from time that could be spent on more exciting or meaningful things. Also, some moves are objectively unhealthy. For example, clients may use substances to regulate emotion, cut themselves, avoid people who are meaningful to them, and so on. These are fairly obvious moves. At the same time, do not forget there are also objectively healthy strategies, such as therapy, meditation, or exercise, that fail to control the inner experience.

ALTERNATIVE TO CONTROL

Addressing creative hopelessness segues into a discussion on whether attempting to control problematic inner experiences is a good idea for clients given everything they have learned from their experiences thus far. We will often say, "After looking at this, I have to wonder, what is the larger problem in your life: that you experience anxiety or that you put this much effort into regulating it?" If the client is unwilling to admit the attempts to control have been unsuccessful, then meet them halfway: "Would you say these attempts at controlling your anxiety have not worked well and have taken a fair amount of time and energy?" Once you feel you and the client are on the same page, suggest an alternative way to solve this issue that does not involve first controlling the inner experience.

We might say, "Most people come in here thinking their anxiety needs to be controlled before they can start living their lives. But what if that isn't totally accurate? There are situations where we can change a thought or a feeling and it's fixed. For example, I might be frustrated with something someone said to me,

I tell them what they said frustrated me, and they respond, 'Oh, sorry, that is not how I meant it at all,' and that changes the feeling. I'm no longer frustrated. But certain things like anxiety about social situations work differently. With anxiety you can't just try harder and get it to change." The following metaphor might help clarify this issue.

Two-games metaphor

You can set this game up for any sport the client likes. I usually ask what some of their favorite sports are to watch and adjust the metaphor to fit their interests.

> Maybe it is more like this, there are two games you can play with regard to your anxiety. The first game is the one you have been playing. It's you and four of your friends against five professional basketball players. The game is played fairly; I mean, there are referees who are neutral. *But the situation here is you are playing to get rid of anxiety.* You can work hard and do your best, but you know your team has no shot at winning this game. Your opponents are just way better than you. So you try, and maybe you make a shot every once in a while, but all and all your team does terribly. That's game one.
>   Game two is different. It is your team against another group of players from your area who are matched with you in ability. This is a fair game. In this game, if your team works hard, puts in a good effort, you will win a fair amount of the time. But you have to put in a good effort to win. *The difference here is that you are playing for quality of life.* You are not playing for more or less anxiety. This can be hard for some people because game one—the game focused on lessening anxiety—will still be going on. The other team will keep playing and scoring. They will try and get you to play. But if you stop paying attention to the game you are in, or send one person over there to try and keep the score under control, you will lose at your current game. You don't get to play both games, and this is where you get to choose. With regard to anxiety, you can either play to control your anxiety or play to have a higher quality of life. I am sure you want both, but trying to have both is part of the reason you are still struggling so much.

Most clients will say they are interested in trying game two but do not understand what that would look like. They might also say not controlling anxiety is "easier said than done." It is prudent to be validating when they say leaving the inner experience alone is difficult: "Yes, I get that letting anxiety be feels like you are not trying or giving up. But maybe this is like letting a baby cry itself to sleep. It is hard, it hurts, it feels wrong, and it is the right move. It's just not the obvious move."

> So here is all I'm asking you to do this week, I would like you to pay attention to the pull to participate in game one and don't give into it a few times.

For just a handful of times, let it stay there and continue on with what you want to be doing with your life. Moving on is important. This is one place where people get stuck. We need to practice living with anxiety. When anxiety shows up, practice allowing it to be present and continuing on with the task you had hoped to do. Maybe you will choose to do a smaller version of the task, and that is fine. Just keep moving your life along.

See "Session 1 homework."

SESSION SUMMARY

In this session you should have learned what the client wants from therapy and what they expect to happen. Using that information, you will have helped them see that, from an ACT standpoint, you and the client are going to focus more on changing behavior than on regulating thoughts, feelings, and emotions. As this is likely different from what the client was originally expecting, you and the client should have agreed to a reasonable duration of therapy to see if it is helpful (again, *helpful* being that the client is living better instead of feeling better) and determined that the client is aware that growth from therapy will be a bit like a rollercoaster. Finally, discussion of creative hopelessness should have helped the client appreciate the difficulty in controlling thoughts, feelings, and bodily sensations; hopefully, this should shift their focus to regulating their actions instead. This week's homework focuses on helping the client see the consequences of attempting to control inner experiences.

REFERENCE

Hayes, S. C., Strosahl, K., & Wilson, K. G. (1999). *Acceptance and commitment therapy: An experiential approach to behavior change.* New York: Guilford Press.

Session 1 Homework

One thing you can do between now and our next session is to observe how you play these games in your daily life. See if you can notice the ways you engage in game one. Because you are not used to doing this, you might not have been aware of all the things you do to moderate, regulate, or solve the issue you're struggling with: distraction, self-blame, talking yourself out of it, avoiding situations, and so on. For ___ [add specific number; 3–5 times] of those times you notice the pull to play game one, practice not listening or giving in to that urge. Just let it be there while you keep doing what you were going to do. The idea is to start practicing how to live your life even when difficult thoughts and feelings show up. Use the following table to keep track of your practice.

	What was the situation where the urge to control/regulate/avoid showed up? (To make this consistent with the question format in the rightmost column)	What did I do with the urge? (To make it consistent with the heading to the right, which is a question)	What was it like to respond in this way?
E.g.:	My friend said something hurtful and I felt bad about myself.	Just let it be there and refocused on our conversation.	Hard to stay present but I was more engaged rather than in my head.
1.			
2.			
3.			
4.			
5.			

Session 2

Control as the Problem

This session is a continuation of what was introduced in the previous session on creative hopelessness. We are still working to help the client see and feel the actual consequences of focusing their time and energy on regulating an inner experience. To reiterate, while control may feel like the right or logical way to handle anxiety (or any internal experience) and may even work to reduce unwanted thoughts and feelings in the short term, in actuality, it probably does not lessen the feeling for a sustained duration, makes it stronger, makes it more central in life, and worsens quality of life. Because ACT is about helping clients move toward their values, not prescribing a specific set of behaviors, it does not preclude effective use of avoidance. That is, avoidance may sometimes be the "right" move for clients, but they need to be able to discriminate when it is and when it is not. We do not tell the client how life works for them. Instead, we want to walk them through their experiences and help them see what is accurate, based on these lived experiences. Again, if regulating the inner experience worked for them, they would not be in therapy. Thus, you are safe guessing that regulating inner experience has the same effect for your client that it has had for all other clients with whom we have worked.

REVIEW HOMEWORK

In the previous session you asked your client to attend to their urges to regulate inner experience and to resist them a few times over the past week. To open this session, let the client generally describe what that was like. However, follow up with questions to elicit specific information on what they learned about their urges to avoid, regulate, or otherwise change their inner experience. Your client has likely never paid much attention to that feeling, so they would not have noticed how they interact with it, let alone tried to interact with it differently. Remember, our verbal abilities allow us to follow *descriptions* of how the world works, even if they do not accurately represent the way it works. We need the client to more fully experience what is going on for them by being aware of what is showing up and attending to thoughts and feelings, rather than denying or looking away from them. Also, discuss with the client what it was like to not give in to anxiety or other inner experiences. How long did the experience stay there? What did it feel like? Was it a good, bad, or neutral experience? Did anything useful come from not giving in? What was being "willing" like? After you and the client have a good understanding of the client's relationship with the target inner experience, follow these next steps to help the client further appreciate their attempts to regulate their inner experience.

CONTROL AS THE PROBLEM

The aim of this set of exercises is to introduce the alternative perspective that attempting to regulate internal experience does more harm than good. We want to move emotional control from an action the client works for or feels good about to something a little more aversive and less rewarding. It is like believing a large, sweet, caffeinated drink is a decent breakfast until someone tells you that it contains over 500 calories and is mostly sugar. The next time you have the opportunity to order one, it might seem less appealing. Similarly, while attempts to control inner experiences may have seemed like a good idea, learning new information about these attempts may alter the client's original assessment of control strategies. Consequently, this new way of looking at the situation changes how rewarding different actions will be for your client.

CONTROL DOES NOT WORK

We like to start with a small discussion about the idea of emotional control before getting into client goals and have the client begin to contemplate the effectiveness of control strategies. By *effective* we mean the following: Do control strategies really help to reduce or eliminate uncomfortable thoughts and feelings? And do they move clients closer to the life they want? The following is a summary of how we would describe it to a client. Note that it is laid out didactically here, as we have omitted client responses; this conversation is typically more of a back-and-forth dialogue than a lecture.

> Last session, we looked at whether controlling your inner experiences was an effective strategy. We made a nice long list of ways you have tried to regulate your anxiety. It seemed almost all of them were effective in the short term—for seconds or minutes. None of them were effective in the long term. If they were, you probably would not be seeing me. But maybe more important, there were some negative results from trying to control so much. It is taking your time and energy. We discussed how this feels like a struggle you

might not be able to keep up for a long time—if you haven't already, you will probably burn out. Finally, we also identified ways of controlling, like isolating yourself, that have been negatively affecting you. All of this leads me to suggest it might be wise to try something different with those inner experiences. Maybe controlling your anxiety is a larger issue than having lots of it. I don't blame you for doing what you have been doing. It makes a lot of sense and is completely reasonable. It is what everyone does, including me. In fact, I would be out of a job if people didn't do this.

Let's walk through some real-life examples.

Tell me situations where controlling thoughts, feelings, or sensations has worked for you. By *worked* I mean you either successfully controlled them or attempting to control them made your life better.

[Discuss times when control has worked, such as distracting for small, difficult events, being motivated by guilt to do the right thing, being motivated by fear to prepare for an important event.]

Yes, when something works in certain situations, it makes sense to try it in other situations. If I have fears about the safety of my vehicle, I get it inspected. When the mechanic says everything is fine, I may no longer experience that fear. Similarly, I had a hand injury and worried I might need surgery. When the doctor told me I should keep exercising with it but to "take it easy," that sure got rid of the worry.

Similarly, there are many other situations in life where we can control things we do not like. Tell me about something you did not like about where you currently live that you changed and are now happier with. For me, I did not like mowing my front lawn or dealing with the weeds that were coming up. So, my partner and I tore up the grass, added dirt mounts, planted lots of water-wise plants, added a drip system, and filled it in with mulch. Now, we have to do about one-tenth the work and spend one-tenth the money on water.

[Discuss with the client things they disliked and were able to fix—even if the fixing took a fair amount of work and time.]

There are many other examples in life. For instance, if you order something at a restaurant and there is a problem with it, what can you do? If you have an event coming up and you need a certain outfit for it, how can you handle that? If you have something that needs to be completed at work and time is tight, how might you get it finished?

I can see how this might be confusing. In so many places in life, if you don't like something, you can change it. It might not be easy, but if you put time into it, you can often change it. But what if our thoughts, feelings, and bodily sensations work according to different rules? If you really look at your experience, you will likely see it is way easier to change things outside your body than inside. Let's see some examples of this.

We typically use a few exercises to illustrate the difficulty of controlling inner experiences. Together, they show the client that (1) we cannot turn off certain feelings at will, (2) we cannot stop a thought from coming into our minds, (3) we cannot turn on certain feelings at will, and (4) we can much more easily do an overt behavior than feel or think something.

Don't feel anxiety

The function of this exercise is to help the client experience how difficult it is to control anxiety. Because the message we get from society, media, family, and friends is, "You can and should control negative feelings," many clients come in believing this. Even when their experience tells them they cannot control anxiety, the rules doled out by their environment can be more persuasive. Thus, we want to make this idea explicit to clients by having them directly contact the difficulty of controlling anxiety through the following exercise.

> If you could have any item in the world (e.g., new car, bike, house), what would you choose? It would be a gift—you don't have to pay for it. [Get the client's answer.] Let's pretend I could actually give that to you but you have to do one thing for me. Here it is: Do not feel anxiety for 30 seconds. Let's pretend I have the magical ability to detect if you feel anxiety. I will know if your emotional state changes—no matter how slightly. Just sit there for the next 30 seconds and don't have anxiety. [Most clients will feel a small change.]

If the client says they did not feel any anxiety, you can ask them what it would be like if they were asked to give a speech in front of a large audience or sing the national anthem at a sporting event. The condition would be the same: Do not feel anxiety.

Don't think of . . .

We have already used anxiety as an example of an inner experience that is difficult to control. Next, we will use the example of a thought. For nearly all people, they will think of whatever you say. There will be a few who say they can stop thoughts. We suggest not arguing with them. On the one hand, it could be true. On the other hand, these clients are probably not getting the point of the exercise or believe thinking about something else counts as not having the first thought (even though a comparison between the two thoughts is needed to ascertain the "absence" of the first thought). Say:

> Whatever thing I say next, I want you to not think of it. I'll offer you the same pretend deal: If you do not think of it, I'll give you that item you would really like. Ready? Don't think of a [name whatever you like].

Sometimes there is something unique to the client or that the client finds funny. All of our clients laugh when we do this exercise. They find it ridiculous. More important, they contact the difficulty of attempting to control a thought.

Create an emotion

We find this next step useful because many of our clients note lack of motivation as a barrier to behavior change. They say, "I could do it if I wasn't so tired," "If I could just get motivated," or "I just need to get some momentum going." What they are saying is, "If I feel a certain emotion, then I can make the change." We totally understand. There are many times in our lives when it is a lot easier to engage in an activity because we are feeling rested, caught up, inspired, or motivated. But as we all know, those emotion are not always there when we would like them to be. Sometimes they are and that is great. However, often they are not, and that is just the way it is. It is dangerous to wait for an emotion to show up before changing behavior. You can illustrate this in many ways, but here is how we like to cover this:

> THERAPIST (T): Thus far, we have talked about stopping an emotion or a thought, but what about creating an emotion? Do you think you could make yourself fall in love with the next person you meet? For example, if I asked you to go out into the hall and feel intense love toward the next person you see, could you do it? [Clients always say no.] Why not?
>
> CLIENT (C): That is something that builds, based on interactions with the person. Maybe I could feel attraction, but not love.
>
> T: Fair. That seems reasonable. Maybe feeling motivated to make the changes we are talking about in this session works the same way. It's like when I have to write a paper or prepare a lecture, I'm never particularly excited to get started—especially on a new project—but once I get rolling I can feel my motivation go up. I start getting into the activity. But which came first: the emotion or action?
>
> C: You did it and then the emotion followed.
>
> T: OK. I think we are on the same page.

Overt behavior

Again, 99% of clients will agree that anxiety and similar inner experiences are difficult to meaningfully control. It is nice to contrast this with something incredibly easy to control: an overt behavior. Asking the client to refrain from touching something in the room for the next minute provides a nice contrast to trying to refrain from thinking or feeling a certain way. We will usually say something like the following:

> Would you agree, trying to control what you think, what emotions you feel, or trying to bring on a certain feeling is pretty difficult? [Allow answer.] I'd like to contrast those actions with another one. See if you can not touch this tissue box for the next minute. [Client will usually laugh.] Are you confident you can keep your hands away from it for the next minute? Controlling things that occur within our bodies is quite different from controlling things that occur outside our bodies.

PULLING IT ALL TOGETHER

After your client has grasped the challenge of attempting to create or regulate internal experiences and contrasted that with the simplicity of regulating overt actions, you may pull all this together for your client. Rather than explaining it all here, read how we would say it to a client.

T: I presented four things I wanted you to accomplish. I asked you to not feel an emotion. Then, I asked you to not think of something I named. Then, I asked you to create an emotion. In all situations you failed and even laughed at the request sometimes.

C: Yes.

T: But it was easy to not engage in the overt action.

C: Correct.

T: I'm not picking on you here. Every person I see does the same thing, but you found it ridiculous for me to ask you to control those things. Your laugh was like, "Nobody could do this." But you did come into therapy specifically asking me to help you regulate your anxiety and fearful thoughts and, in some way, help you feel motivated to do this. I wonder if our culture has taught us that anxiety can and should be controlled and there is something wrong with you if you cannot accomplish this. But when we look at it together in this room, controlling thoughts and feelings and creating motivation are actually exceedingly difficult. What if that is really the way things work?

C: Then what are we supposed to do here?

T: Do you remember how easy it was to control your actions? Maybe it is more about changing what you do than about changing what you feel or think. This is an age-old discussion in psychology: Do your thoughts and feelings cause your behavior, or do your behaviors cause your thoughts and feelings? You can guess which side of that debate I fall on.

WHY ARE PEOPLE SO FOCUSED ON CONTROL?

In an attempt to undermine the rule that thoughts and feelings need to be regulated in order to live a healthy life, discuss with your client what led them to believe inner experiences are bad and need to be controlled. Every client has a different past that led them to believe this area of life needs to be controlled.

Helping the client become aware of the function of those societal institutions or particular people will hopefully alter their effect on the client outside of the session. This is because exploring sources that have instilled in clients a habit of emotional control may undermine the influence of those sources by beginning to question their premise.

It is like following the rule that you cannot swim for at least 3 hours after a meal but not being able to explain why you do so until someone explicitly asks about it. Then, you realize the only reason is, "because my parents told me not to," and your behavior is not actually based on reading reports or learning from almost drowning. That is what we are hoping for: We want the client to view suggestions about emotional control more skeptically. Furthermore, this discussion normalizes our adherence to emotional control: All of us do it because we have been taught to do so by the world around us. The following are common sources from which people learn about emotional control. Ask the client what these groups have taught them about emotional control

1. Family (parents, siblings, grandparents, spouses, etc.)
2. Media (e.g., TV, news reporting)
3. Medical professionals and advertisements for medication
4. Friends
5. Past therapists

As this conversation wraps up, remind the client, "Maybe your biggest problem is not the inner experience but how hard you try to control it." The conversation might go like this:

T: Can you think of times in your life when people taught you certain thoughts or feelings are bad?

C: There are a couple that stand out to me. Both involved getting hurt. In one situation, I tripped and fell down the stairs. It knocked the wind out of me. My dad said, "You're fine. Get up and get ready for school." I remember being really confused. And this happened lots of times. I'd get hurt, and instead of a hug or checking on me I was told, "You're fine."

T: Those are solid examples. How about from other people? Maybe examples from people you consider really caring and nurturing?

C: My mom is a very caring person, but she certainly hates to see me sad or upset. She would pretty much do anything to keep me from feeling sad. It's really sweet in a way, but she sacrificed a lot so that we could feel "positive."

T: Neat. And what about society?

C: I don't know.

T: I mean restaurants, businesses, drug companies, and so on. Do you have any thoughts about other areas that are less personal?

C: Drug companies are pretty clearly out there to help us regulate. I do get a kick out of advertising and the way they show happy people doing every-thing. I'm always thinking, "I've never seen someone who looks and acts like that in my life!"

T: This is fun. I just wanted you to get a sense of the world we are living in. It's pretty clear, the things we are working on in here don't really match with some of the things taught in the outside world.

Remind clients it is not their fault

We like to provide context for why someone might get into this pattern of action. It makes sense that someone would believe they can control their inner experiences when so many people and institutions tell them they can, when control works so well in other areas of life, when there are times emotional control does work, or when they do not quite appreciate the limited success of short-term control strategies. Talk to your client about their context, using language as follows.

> I just want to chat with you a little bit about why people get into these situations where they work so hard to regulate an inner experience. There are many reasons. A main one is what we just discussed. People and groups we trust and respect have led us to believe we can and should regulate thoughts and feelings we don't like. For example, if I tell my wife I am feeling frus-trated with something at work, she will try to make me feel better. She will ask me what is going on, offer solutions on how to solve it, or give me other ways to look at the situation. If I told my mom I was nervous about asking my boss for a raise, I am sure she would say something like, "Well, I am sure you will be kind and professional when asking. What's the worst that can happen? I also think you are doing a great job and likely deserve it." These are very kind things to say, but they suggest on some level that I need to feel something other than frustration or anxiety, that frustration and anxiety are "bad" states. It would almost be weird if my wife said, "Yes, work can really be frustrating. How is it to feel frustrated?" Or if she said, "I bet those are very interesting emotions you feel in that situation. Let's talk about them."
>
> Also, in so many other situations in life, if you don't like something, you can change it. For example, when my hair grows too long, what do you think I do? If I had a lot of weeds growing in my flowerbeds, what can I do about it? If the paint was peeling off my house, what should I do? But if we go back to my examples earlier, if I was feeling nervous about asking my boss for a raise, what easy solution do I have? Maybe because we can so easily regulate

things outside our bodies, we don't realize the same strategies don't work as well with things inside our bodies.

It also gets complicated because we are sometimes able to control what happens inside our bodies. For example, if I am frustrated with my children, I might ask my wife if she can be in charge for a bit and then go do something else. Ten minutes later, I feel less frustrated. Similarly, when I am at the dentist, they have a television on the ceiling so I can watch it while they are cleaning my teeth and it is a nice distraction from the scraping. I distract myself most of the way through my dental appointments and it makes them easier to get through. Maybe emotional control works well briefly in relatively unimportant situations, but when we really get into more intense emotions, like with an anxiety disorder, they are out of our control. *Control might be one of those things that only works well in certain situations, and we have to pay attention to what those situations are.*

OFFER ACCEPTANCE AS AN ALTERNATIVE

There has been a lot of discussion on what the definition of acceptance is. The actual definition is in Chapter 1, but it seems worth offering a working definition for you and the client. *Acceptance* is finding a place within where all inner experiences can exist. There are two important parts to think about. First, acceptance is not just for the "negative" inner experiences—we practice acceptance of all inner experiences; it is just easier with "positive" ones. Second, acceptance is not a means to regulate emotions; acceptance of all inner experiences is the goal.

Scholars have talked about tolerance as a means to eventual reductions in unpleasant inner experiences. In contrast to acceptance, tolerance describes a more reluctant or begrudging stance toward inner experiences; in many ways, it is conditional. If clients say, "I can accept feeling anxious if it goes away after a period of time" or "I can make room for anxiety if it will go away in the long-run," they are referring to tolerance. Acceptance as we mean it is unconditional. It is about genuinely welcoming difficult thoughts and feelings into your life even if you do not like them, just as you would love your pet even if they chewed up your favorite shoes. Clients can define the parameters of the situation in which the inner experiences show up, but they cannot restrict what and how much shows up if they are practicing acceptance. Moreover, while there is certainly evidence for the short-term effectiveness of tolerance, there is also notable evidence that while certain inner experiences may diminish, they never go away. There is no unlearning, only new learning. Thus, fears, anxieties, thoughts, and memories may fade, but they return under certain circumstances. They may not be as large or as powerful, but for some people merely experiencing them again means failure.

The idea of acceptance as an end in itself may be obvious once we think about it but less obvious in our day-to-day lives. We have tens of thousands of thoughts a day. We would argue, people do nothing with the vast majority of them. Even writing this, random thoughts about food, time, responsibilities, cleaning, and other things have shown up and I (M.P.T.) have done nothing with any of those. I sort of noticed that they occurred and refocused on writing. But with each one, I had a moment when I could choose to do something about them. I could have found something to eat, started getting ready for my next appointment, worked on other things, or cleaned my office. These were relatively unimportant thoughts to me, so they were pretty easy to let them be, though it might have been more difficult to let a more meaningful thought just be. We also have those really powerful or scary thoughts that feel impossible to just let be there. We feel like something needs to be done about them. What is important is, with practice, we get better at letting any thought just be there. Letting thoughts be can become second nature, even with very difficult thoughts. Here is how we like to introduce this idea to a client:

> I think you have tried really hard to deal with your situation and you have done the best you can with the way things work. I'd give you an A for effort. But what if we could move that effort over to something else that works a lot better? Here is a small but odd example of what I am getting at. You know I'm an academic, right? So writing papers is a big part of my job. When I started graduate school, I did not know how to type. I stared at the keyboard and found one key at a time. I'd argue that I tried really hard to type my papers. Then one day, I decided I just needed to learn to type and looked up how to online. I typed even more slowly for a month or two, using the correct method before I was back at my original speed. Now, 15 years later, I'm probably four times faster because I taught myself that. I had to take a few steps backward in terms of speed, but the lifelong benefit has been huge.
>
> What if we are in a similar situation here? I see you've put a lot of effort into your issue but I think you are doing it in an ineffective way—or at least not the most effective way. I can show you a new way. It will be difficult, you will feel clumsy, and it will feel like your old way is easier. All this is true. You will be better at your old way of handling it, but your old way is likely not the most effective long-term strategy.
>
> If trying really hard to regulate your unwanted inner experience has gotten you to this place, then it is possible a totally different strategy might make sense. I've been at this for a long time, and very few people come to this conclusion on their own. I think that is partly why so many people struggle with difficult thoughts and feelings and why psychologists stay in business: because what is helpful seems illogical.
>
> Let me demonstrate with an example. [Take a small piece of paper and have the client write on it the inner experience they are struggling with. Then, ask the client to hold up one hand. Put the paper between your hand and theirs. Then push. Ask the client to try and keep that inner experience away from them. Keep pushing. Remind them how important it is to keep it away from them.]
>
> How much work is this? Are you getting a little tired? Do you think you could do this all day? Doesn't this feel a little similar to what you are already

doing, working really hard to keep this thing away? [Ask the client to stop pushing. Gather the card and ask the client to just sit there and do nothing. Toss the card on the client's lap. It should be just sitting on the client's lap.]

In both situations, the card was touching you. Which one requires more work? Maybe we could interact with your inner experience in this way. We could be in contact with the feeling and not do anything about it. If you are willing to take this a step further, I suggest taking that piece of paper, folding it up, and putting it in your pocket. You will carry it around all day like you do with other inner experiences. Sometimes you will bump into it and other times you will forget about it. When you take it out tonight, don't throw it away. Maybe put it back in your pocket tomorrow.

Practicing willingness

Although we are teaching acceptance in this phase, the term *acceptance* has a lot of baggage. Thus, we use the term *willingness* with clients. Acceptance connotes tolerance or resignation to most people. They also confuse it with accepting how things are in the world, which is not necessarily what we are advocating. We actually teach that things in the world are more changeable than things within oneself. Specifically, we want to empower clients to change things within their control (e.g., behaviors) in the presence of internal barriers outside of their control (e.g., fear)—not to live life passively. We would say the following:

Allowing that thought, feeling, or bodily sensation to be present without trying to change or control it is what I call willingness. It means making a choice to allow something to be there. It is an action—something you do. It is not an attitude or an emotional stance. Your emotions and thoughts might be all over the place, but you get to choose how to treat those emotions. You can choose to be kind to them, find a way for them to be there, or find a way for them to come and go. I like to think of them as annoying houseguests or coworkers. You don't have to like the person to be nice to them. You might even hate the person *and* you can be polite to them if doing so is consistent with the kind of person you want to be. These emotions and thoughts are kind of like that. They will show up, you may dislike them, and you can be kind to them and allow them to have a home within you if that helps you pursue the life you want for yourself.

Distinguishing between liking and allowing

Sometimes, the internal event that the client is struggling with is disturbing. An emotion like depression or worry about finances may not be that objectively disturbing, but a traumatic memory or an obsession about violence toward loved ones—as in OCD—might feel different to your client. In these circumstances it is worth discussing what you are asking the client to accept. You are asking the client to accept thoughts, feelings, memories, and bodily sensations—not the occurrence of trauma or acts of violence. They are struggling with unwanted *thoughts* about these things, and thoughts about events are different from the actual events. This is still not easy to practice, especially when clients have bought into the content of these thoughts because the thoughts feel as real as the events themselves. It is important for you as a therapist to appreciate the hard work your client is doing, even if you can see these thoughts as just thoughts. Here is how we might say this using a traumatic memory as an example.

> I have an uncomfortable feeling about asking you to allow thoughts about that car wreck to be there. I can't imagine how difficult it is to have that memory. And I also know offering to really make that thought go away or be different is not fair, because we both know that's not possible. That is not how these types of thoughts work; your experience tells you this. These thoughts don't just go away, so we need to find a way for them to show up without knocking us off course or ruining our day. First, let's notice what this experience is: the memory of the trauma, pictures of the trauma that show up in your head. We are not talking about the actual trauma. Could you notice these memories as images floating by in your mind? When you stop trying to push them out, can you notice what they can actually do to you? Do these images really have the power to stop you from living your life? Do you want your life to be controlled by these images? What has been the cost of your running? What have you given up in life to avoid these images? Has it been worth it?

Acceptance is a choice

Acceptance is something we choose to do. It is a way of responding to real or anticipated internal events. Our clients might not want to be willing. They may not feel motivated to act that way. That is OK, because being willing is an action, and we can choose to engage in most actions regardless of whether we feel like it. Moreover, like many actions, we may not be that good at accepting the first time we try it. The more we work at it, the better at it we get. In addition, a little guidance from an expert can help us do it better. We like to use the example of a coach. Here is what we might say to a client:

> Being willing is something you do. It is an action. This is good, because we can engage in actions no matter what we are feeling. Some days we have lots of energy and some day we don't. Regardless, we can work on being more willing every day. Like most new things we do, we will not be good at it at first. Give me an example of something you are learning or just learned. [Discuss with the client the process of getting better at things over time.] Yes,

just like that, I expect you to struggle mightily at first, but over time I bet you will get better and better at this. I like to think of this like when I learned how to kick a soccer ball. I remember kicking and getting better and better. Then my brother, who is actually good at soccer, started to give me some tips. I started being able to control where the ball went. The ball moved faster. I eventually learned how to make the ball bend. I am not sure I would have figured out those more advanced things accidentally. I think I needed some expert guidance to really get that good. So maybe our work will be like that. There is a skill you can learn, it will take a while, and I will be coaching you.

DOING IT

Every session from now on, we will practice the area(s) of psychological flexibility discussed in session. These behavioral commitments have two purposes: (1) to pursue valued activities and (2) to practice psychological flexibility in real-world situations. It is important to help the client be aware of each area of growth as they move forward. Sometimes the client will be more caught up in the enjoyment of meaningful action. But when that engagement is not there, ask the client to focus on practicing psychological flexibility. For example, if I was at a boring talk I thought would be helpful but was not, I could use the time to practice being present and not getting caught up in my negative thoughts about the lecture. We are early in discussion of the six ACT processes of change, but we are already working on acceptance and have touched on defusion. Values and behavioral commitments are easy to introduce in the exercise described next. We are going to build on this behavioral commitment at each session, but because this is the first one, we will start simply.

Work with the client to find a small behavior change they can practice a few times over the next week. We describe homework in more detail at the end of the chapter. In addition, it might be helpful to preemptively identify possible internal barriers that might show up: anxiety, laziness, thoughts of "this is too hard." The idea is to set clients up for success as much as possible. Note that these behaviors should serve as progressive steps toward a larger pattern of valued living, and the ultimate goal is for clients to engage in a meaningful network of actions. The idea is once clients start doing things that matter to them, they will encounter the intrinsically rewarding elements of living a life consistent with their chosen values and be able to elaborate on these actions in a sustainable way.

Motivational description for client

This basic exercise can be adapted to just about any client. Every client has something they have worked toward, so alter this exercise to fit their situation. For example, if you are at a college counseling center, use college. If you are associated with the military, use engagement in the military. If you are a religious counselor, build on aspects of engaging with your religion. We are going to use college as that is where we work.

> You came in here because some inner experience is getting in the way. I am hoping to work with you to learn how to handle it differently—hopefully, more effectively. Let's use something important to you as an example. Would you say graduating from college is important to you? Graduating from college is a long haul. There is a lot to learn about many different topics—not just classes but studying, making friends, extracurricular activities, how much to study and what to study, and the list goes on. Building skills in each of these areas will help the whole thing. But there are some general skills that will help across all these aspects of college. I think of the work we do in session as working on the general skills that are helpful everywhere in college, and the specific exercises you pick each week apply to individual activities. No one thing you will work on in college will cause you to graduate, but each thing you get better at will contribute to your graduation. Each week, we will work on a little thing that will help with your life, and as we put all these skills together, you will get closer to your goal.

WRAP UP WITH HOMEWORK: WEEKLY BEHAVIORAL COMMITMENT

Each week, you will have the client engage in one behavioral commitment. This is one of the six processes of change. The actual commitment will vary depending on the client, how far along they are in therapy, and what their main presenting problem is. These commitments can occur multiple times a day (e.g., eat more fruits and vegetables), daily (e.g., smoke 15 cigarettes a day instead of 20), or weekly (e.g., interact with a particular person). They can even be on a different schedule, such as to pull zero hairs for three full days over the next week for a client diagnosed with trichotillomania. We are not going to specify actual behavioral commitments because every client requires individualized behavior change exercises. Most lines of work have already developed behavior change procedures. Think of ACT as making it more likely that behavior change will occur. In line with this aim, there are a few points to consider when setting behavioral commitments in ACT more broadly:

1. The behavior(s) should be concrete. There should be no question as to whether it occurred or not. For example, "be more social" is too vague. Instead you might work with your client to define the behavior as "agree to one social interaction a day that involves at least three sentences spoken."

2. There should be a very high chance the behavior will occur. We like to say we want a 90% chance it will occur. If it is not at 90% chance of occurring, make it easier.

3. The behavioral commitments are based on how difficult the person finds the task; they are not based solely on how much emotion the event creates. They are more a gauge of how big a step the client can *successfully* make.

4. The amount of emotion that occurs during the behavioral commitment is secondary. We engage in the event and then look back and see what the event was like. When a client practices acceptance and defusion, events that normally create a lot of emotion might no longer have that effect. Similarly, events that do not typically create emotion may create quite a lot.

5. The action should be tied to clients' values in some way. Sometimes the link is very clear (e.g., inviting a friend to hang out for the value of social connection) and other times the client will just practice to build skills that will help them follow their values in the future.

6. The homework should allow for practice of a specific process of change during the behavioral commitment. The process of change you are targeting should be made explicit for your client. Hence, in framing the homework, state what skill the client should be attending to as they engage in the valued action. For example: "As you talk to your friend this week, I want you to just notice the feelings of annoyance or frustration, notice where they show up in your body, and what they feel like. Practice simply observing them without listening to them, and acting kindly toward your friend."

7. Allow for flexibility in the specific behavioral commitment. The broader goal is for the client to practice certain skills and move toward their values. Therefore, if the client's original behavioral commitment is to go for a hike, but it rains, they can watch a nature documentary (if the value is connecting with nature) or go to the gym (if the value is physical health) instead.

Here is some language you can use to describe this.

To provide some structure, we will be using this worksheet (refer to *Behavioral Commitment Worksheet*, Appendix C) to track your behavioral commitments every week. You'll see from this worksheet that we don't care just about what action you're committing to but also why you're doing it, what skills you're building, and how you'll navigate barriers that might show up. We'll also identify ways to set yourself up for success, like setting reminders or having accountability buddies. So, what would be an important or meaningful action you could realistically work on this week? Remember, we want the chance of your successfully completing the action to be around 90%. We think of this as taking a step toward your larger goals.

SESSION SUMMARY

By the end of this session, you and your client should be on the same page about the long-term ineffectiveness of control strategies and the consequences of excessively using them. In addition, your client should have a working understanding of willingness so they can begin practicing this skill as part of their homework. You will have walked them through experiential exercises and metaphors about acceptance. At the end of the session, you and your client should have decided on homework they will be doing over the next week.

6

Sessions 3 and 4

Acceptance Supported by Defusion

Thus far, you should have spent time helping your client understand three things: (1) inner experiences are hard to control and attempting to do so may actually exacerbate the struggle; (2) it is normal to try and control inner experiences because there is a lot of social pressure to do so and control works in many other situations; and (3) *willingness* to let inner experiences simply be there could be a useful way to handle them, because willingness allows one to pursue what is important to them without needing to first change something inside them. Complete the ACT ADVISOR (see Figure 2.2) again to see where they are on the six ACT processes of change. If you and your client are not on the same page, go over the processes again experientially. Do not tell the client what they should think. Instead, walk through the basic material from the first two sessions again before going back to acceptance, using key exercises and metaphors. Your job is not to convince the client, and watch for the urge to over-explain or argue. Many clients easily shift back into old patterns, and hearing this information again helps it to sink in, particularly if they can connect it with their own personal experience and what has worked and not worked in their life.

GREETING THE CLIENT

Most of us naturally ask our clients, "How are you?" or "How was your week?" at the start of our sessions. There is nothing wrong with these questions per se. The issue is you will usually get an answer that has something to do with how they felt that week. It would be natural for a client to say something like, "Pretty good; I was not that anxious" or "It was a rough week; my anxiety was high." An answer like this tells you the client is still not on board with how ACT conceptualizes inner experiences. If the client answers in this way, they still believe happiness is the lack of particular inner experiences. This is a dangerous stance to have because your client's inner experiences are going to fluctuate throughout life. If the client answers in this fashion, it is a great opportunity to discuss their stance toward inner experiences, which might go something like the following:

> I want to discuss something with you. I asked you how your week went and you told me about your anxiety levels. Why did you focus on that?
>
> Tell me about how you see your anxiety levels playing into whether you had a good week or not.
>
> If we go back to some of the conversations we've had, we were talking about the effects of attempting to control or regulate your anxiety. Have you been successful at that?
>
> Many of us believe we can only do the things we want in life when anxiety is below a certain threshold. Heck, that is what pretty much everyone in the world has been saying to us. But what if that model is wrong? What if we first do the things we want in life and our inner experiences follow? If the situation is scary, we will feel scared. If it's fun, we'll feel excited. If there is a chance of things going wrong, we will feel anxiety. The emotion comes after the action, and people generally find they have a lot more control over what they do than what they feel. So let's talk about what you did this week. This is partly my fault with how I worded the question. I will start asking you how *engaged you were this week,* and you can tell me what you did and what you worked on. I would like to hear about your successes and failures—in terms of the things you did rather than what you felt. With that in mind, what did you work on this week?

Now it is up to you to ask questions at the opening of the session that have more to do with what the client has worked on over the week and less on how they felt. We think this type of conversation is useful because it frames the way the client looks at things. Remember: You are one of the few people in your client's life who sees things like this, and you need to keep reinforcing that viewpoint every chance you get—you are up against many people who are teaching otherwise.

REVIEW HOMEWORK

In the last session, you asked the client to agree to a set number of behavioral commitments tied to their values. They were not huge commitments. We wanted the commitments to be linked to the client's values so there would be some motivation to make these changes and so the client could experience the life benefits from engaging in meaningful actions. We also want the client to practice building psychological flexibility. Thus, when discussing the homework with the client, focus on these two things: (1) "How was it to do things you care about?" and (2) "Psychologically (or internally), what was it like to try and make these changes?"

Do not try to convince the client it was wonderful to follow their values. It might not have been all that great. We want the client to come into contact with the effects of their actions so their behavior can be shaped by their actual experiences rather than by rules about how things should work. Before starting therapy, much of their behavior was likely about emotional avoidance. We want them to contact the effects of engaging in life. Sometimes this will be really fun and other times it will not. Your openness will allow them to feel free to try things and give you honest reports. Thus, if they can honestly say actions tied to their values were not all that great, that is good to know. Try something different the next week because if they do not connect with the purpose of the behavioral commitment, they will not maintain behavior change.

Hopefully, as you move along through the course of ACT, the client will start to see the value of being more psychologically flexible. Not only will it allow the client to engage in new actions that are important to them, but they should also be more comfortable in their day-to-day actions. Remember, building values and behavioral commitments will make acceptance and defusion easier and more meaningful. Similarly, stronger skills with acceptance and defusion will allow the client to engage more and more comfortably with whatever they are working on.

A TIP FOR DOING ACT: BE EXPERIENTIAL

ACT is supposed to be an experiential therapy. The concepts and lessons from ACT are taught more effectively with real-life situations. They can be events from the past week, things from a while ago, or events happening in session. Rather than using a hypothetical situation to teach a concept, use a recent event with some emotion still tied to it. I like to joke, "There is a reason there is a tissue box in every therapy room: because talking about sad events causes us to feel the emotions from that event." It is an interesting line to say, because it may help the client refrain from judging themselves for having a particular emotion. It also highlights that talking about emotion-laden events will likely result in experiencing those emotions in session.

The reason we are bringing this up is that the client will likely describe events from the week that went well or poorly. In both situations, there are opportunities to talk about emotions that were present and how the client dealt with them. If you handle this well and spend some time talking about the events and what they were like, the client will experience some emotion that was present during the events. This is useful because it either makes the discussion about how they handled that emotion more real or provides an experiential opportunity to talk about these issues. You can sometimes take these conversations further experientially by also exploring with clients what it is like to discuss these issues with you right now, shifting the focus to what is happening right now in the room and in relation to your interactions with each other. As you get more comfortable with ACT, you can jump into it whenever it occurs. For now, save these events in your mind and use them when you are having a discussion later. Here is just a quick example of what we are getting at. In the following example, the client and therapist are discussing acceptance.

THERAPIST (T): Could we spend a few minutes on how you are dealing with these self-critical thoughts? I think there might be a way to make them a little easier on you. Tell me again about the struggle you were having at work this week with your new coworker.

CLIENT (C): Yes. He's new and young. Which is great because there is a lot of energy, but he also talks down to me. He explains things I already know, and if I try and interrupt him to say I understand this topic already, he just keeps going because he says this is different.

T: This is a really helpful example. Tell me more about it.

C: OK, it gets my self-critical thoughts going. I wonder why he automatically perceives me this way. I wonder why I can't tell him to stop. I wish someone would ask for my advice or opinion at some point.

T: How does all this make you feel?

C: It makes me feel frustrated with myself.

T: What else?

If the therapist continued to dig deeper and discuss this, the client would likely start to feel the emotions they are struggling with. Two more minutes on this topic and the client would really feel it.

T: Do you feel that way now?

C: Yes, I am putting myself down for being stuck on this. I'm like, why can't you handle this? This is just an annoying coworker. Everyone has them. Geez.

T: I hear you. I do. If this has been around for a long time—and I believe it has—would you be willing to handle it differently? Instead of treating these self-critical thoughts as though they are meaningful—like if they were coming from your boss or your mom—could we treat them as though they were coming from an announcer at a sporting event? Announcers just keep talking whether you want them to or not. And if you get too caught up in what the announcer is saying you might miss out on the game. Maybe you can treat these thoughts in your head like an extra negative announcer at a sporting event.

C: But they feel so real.

T: They do. This announcer really wants your attention. This one is good. There will be times to listen to him, but there are other times when he can just be ignored. Actually, there might be lots of times when he can be ignored.

The point of this description is not to suggest you use this analogy but to help you see how you can link the client's responses from homework into material you will cover later in session.

ACCEPTANCE AGAIN

Two issues generally show up when addressing acceptance. First, acceptance of inner experiences is not something with which most clients have experience. Therefore, it is likely they will have lost touch with your discussion about acceptance from last week. In our experience, the client's connection with actual acceptance lasts for maybe a day or two at this point. There is too much pressure from the outside world to regulate their inner experiences. Furthermore, the client likely also has some long-held belief that if they try hard enough, they will be able to regulate or control their interfering inner experiences. It is difficult to give up this belief.

Second, the client probably experiences the difficult thoughts, feelings, or bodily sensations as scary—even terrifying at times. Thus, the idea of just letting them be there is counterintuitive. Clients often feel like they need to be doing something because, even if it is not working, they feel like they are at least trying. We have heard clients say things like, "You expect me to sit here and do nothing about it?" We understand where that feeling comes from, but that type of belief is based on an inaccurate rule. It is sort of like saying, "You don't want me to comfort my baby. You want me to let him fall asleep all by himself?" Sometimes what our minds tell us is right is not what is actually going to work best. The client has been engaged in the control agenda for so long that they cannot see another option and the inner experience is perceived as so threatening that allowing it to just be there is unfathomable.

One of the interesting things about how cognition works is that our thoughts are sometimes experienced like the real event. When a client worries about a negative future event, they might feel real anxiety about that event. When they think about a past sad event, they might feel depression. If they remember a trauma, they might feel fear. Even if the feeling is less intense, it is still there. The mind experiences these cognitions as if they were much more real than they actually are. We often say to our clients, "I am not asking you to be willing to have the trauma that happened to you. I am asking you if you can be willing to have a memory about the trauma." When fusion is still high, acceptance will be hindered. Acceptance and defusion are tied together because it is difficult to accept things that appear truly scary and dangerous. With defusion in place, the client can hopefully recognize the inner experiences for what they are: thoughts, conditioned emotions, bodily sensations. Therefore, when acceptance is covered this second time, we like to review it and intertwine defusion.

Talk to clients about trying acceptance again

As we just noted, the client might have struggled with implementing acceptance. They likely tried it and either found the whole thing too overwhelming or worked at it for a short while before shifting back to their previous methods of emotional control. If you have not already discussed it during the homework review, talk to the client about how they responded to their difficult inner experiences over the week. There will be examples from homework and their day-to-day activities. It is important to have this conversation so you can use examples from the client's life to talk about acceptance. The only way you will know which elements of acceptance were difficult for them is through talking to them about it. We will offer some general guidance on how to go over acceptance again. The descriptions and exercises are general and tackle many issues that occur when trying to implement acceptance.

General description of acceptance

Acceptance is about finding a way to objectively notice all inner experiences and consciously deciding how to respond to them. Inner experiences are not good or bad; they are just indicators that something is going on. Sometimes it is a good idea to respond to inner experiences and other times, not so much. Take hunger, for example—for many people, eating and hunger are not perfectly correlated. We experience the feeling of hunger and, depending on a number of variables, we decide what makes the most sense to do. I (M.P.T.) have literally eaten at a burger place and felt hunger for a second meal. The feeling of hunger was there, but I did not need to act on that feeling. I often say at workshops, "When I feel love toward my wife, acting on that emotion has never gone wrong." Theoretically, there could be times when it would not make sense, like calling my wife from a meeting to tell her I love her. However, in my experience, it has always worked out to act on that feeling. We want the client to have the ability to have any inner experience and have the flexibility to do whatever they want in that moment. Then, when anxiety, depression, pain, fear, or other inner experiences show up, the client can still follow their values. Here is what I would say if I was seeing a client for a second time and they had just practiced being more accepting and were struggling with it.

Being willing is an interesting thing. It involves treating all internal events openly and skeptically. Some things that occur within our bodies are very informative, whereas a whole bunch of events that occur in our bodies mean nothing. Just take 30 seconds and sit there and see what shows up in your mind. Even in the brief time we have just been talking I have had thoughts about work I have to do, how I'm hungry, how much time is left, asking myself if this is going well . . . and that was just in the past minute.

Your mind will throw out thoughts all day long. I'm going to estimate that 90% of them are basically meaningless observations of the world. It's like an announcer talking about the things you see. Our issue is, certain thoughts or feelings show up and they really grab us. For some clients it's body image, for others it's worthlessness, and for others it's fear that something bad might happen in the future. The thought just before about needing a haircut was no biggie and then—BOOM—that thought about your weight shows up and everything comes to a halt. For some reason, your mind has decided that thought is worth listening to. You can't just see this thought like the other ones. It gets special attention. But why? Does it have to?

I would like you to practice treating all thoughts as just things that pop up in our heads. This will be super easy with certain thoughts and way harder with other ones. But at the core, they are all just thoughts. This will certainly take practice. Being willing is a skill like any other activity that you do.

School teacher analogy

Maybe it is a little like this: let's say you volunteer at an elementary school. If you have children, you can imagine being in one of the rooms. If you don't, think of doing a friend a favor and helping out in a room for a few hours. I don't know if you have ever been in an elementary school room but they are a controlled-chaos sort of thing. Most teachers have excellent control over the room, but in every classroom I have been in there is still a bit of madness going on. Even if the kids follow along really well and do what is asked of them, they still do odd things from time to time. For example, one kid might hit another kid. I've seen kids raise their hands and say crazy things. One time, I saw a kid raise his hand and after the teacher called on him, he said, "We got a new cat." The teacher didn't reinforce that action; she just moved on to the next raised hand. I've seen kids wander around the classroom, or walk up to the whiteboard and try and help the teacher, or fight, or argue; the list goes on. I am sure there are students the teachers love and others they really dislike. Yes, teachers yell, but they are also sweet, patient, and respectful, and, above all, they work with our children every day to make them better and more talented little kids.

Pretend the kids are your inner experiences and you are the teacher. Some thoughts or emotions are doing what you would like and some are not. You can do things to affect them but you don't have total control over them. You love some of the thoughts and you wish some would move away or go to another classroom. Yet, all you can really do is arrange things the best you can and then be patient with what you can't control. I would also imagine teachers stay in contact with their values throughout the day. I've asked some, and they have goals such as get every student to "grade level" on tests. Other have goals such as helping their students be "successful" in their lives. Some speak about building self-esteem in the kids. No matter what it is about, they are working toward something meaningful—something they value. If the teacher can stay in contact with that value, there is always a clear move in terms of teaching, no matter how well or poorly behaved the students are. How might you be like the teacher, and how might your inner experiences be like these students?

ACCEPTANCE NEEDS DEFUSION TO WORK

Acceptance is deeply dependent on defusion. Defusion is the skill of being able to see inner experiences for what they are. A thought is only sounds and pictures in one's head, a feeling is just bodily reactions along with cognitions, and physiological sensations are more intense bodily reactions occurring at unexpected times. If we go back to the introduction chapter (Chapter 1), recall that fusion is the result of being able to respond to one event in terms of another and how the impact of those events changes accordingly. This is a life-enriching and life-saving ability. You only need to look at something that might be dangerous to feel fear and surmise you should handle the situation more cautiously. You can also learn through direction and instruction. Our verbal abilities allow us to effectively respond in many situations by making sense from cues in the environment and allowing us to experience emotions appropriate for that situation. We do not need to wait for real consequences. We "get it" immediately.

For example, if I sense my partner is feeling down, I can go through options of how to improve their day. Given every little thing going on in our lives, I can think of what would most likely make them happy. I can predict how they will respond to an event we have never encountered. This same ability also allows me to experience what it would be like to get fired, lose a loved one, or be seriously injured. These have never happened to me but I can sense what they would be like. As therapists, we get a lot of training and opportunities to learn how to not get entangled in these types of thoughts, but many of our clients have not learned this. When something in their world cues one of these thoughts, they experience it as real and powerful, and partially because of the power they give the thought, they get pulled into doing something about it. Defusion provides separation between the inner experience and everything that comes with it. The inner experience still occurs, but the client is able to see it as sounds in the head and sensations in the body—not as the event itself. When a thought is just a thought, it is easy to make room for it. When it is perceived as real, it makes sense to do everything we can to avoid it. Here is how we might first introduce this to a client.

> Having language is a blessing and a curse. Language has allowed us to live in luxury compared to all other things on this planet. Look around. We are in a nice room, the temperature is what we want, we are safe, and we have everything we need. There is a restroom right down the hall. We have a whiteboard right here so we can write things down and talk about them. Heck, even the walls are insulated so sound does not travel between rooms. This is set up just as we need it. We can thank language for the ability to set this up. Because of language, humans have done amazing things. Our life expectancy keeps increasing. We have lots of interesting things such as movies, music,

delicious food, and the list goes on. Without language, we could not have accomplished all this.

But the curse of language is, I can ask you right now to tell me about something horrible or unfair that happened to you and, even though it might have happened many years ago, you will feel sadness or guilt about this event. You might even tear up or cry—not that crying is bad. Just notice that language allows us to experience events that are not happening right now—or maybe never even happened—just through talking or thinking about them. I am sure you have had the experience of being in bed ready to go to sleep, when you think about something unfortunate that happened to you—or might happen to you. Boom. Now you are lying in bed with an anxious feeling, even though you are totally safe in that moment.

This is the power of language. If we want to enjoy its benefits, we have to deal with the problems that come with it. If we want to live comfortably, we also have to experience fear, doubt, depression, and anxiety—even when they are unwarranted. Without language, we would just be in the moment such that when we are fed, warm, dry, and safe, we would be pretty stable emotionally. We might feel fear at times, but we would not be anxious. However, the same thing that allows us to feel anxiety also tells us to save money for retirement—and allows us to daydream about retirement. There is no surgery we can get or medicine we can take to change how this works. This is what human minds do. Our work is to figure out how to respond to this process.

Once you have laid the groundwork for how thoughts work and the utility of defusion, discuss with your client times when the mind is really helpful and times when it is not. Most of us can easily think of when it saved us from a problem or made life better, but we can also think of times when it did the opposite.

T: As I said earlier, the mind is going at all times. It has something to say about everything. I often use this little example to help show our minds cannot just let something be. It will judge, evaluate, criticize, predict, plan, and so on. Again, this ability is a blessing and a curse. It allows us to do wonderful things. It also allows us to do horrible things and torture ourselves in the midst of plenty. Look around this room and see if there is anything you are unfamiliar with.

C: There is that electronic thing on the ceiling.

T: OK, guess what it is.

C: I would think it has something to do with Wi-Fi or maybe a fire alarm system.

T: Look around the room some more and see if there is anything you can't name.

C: I can pretty much name everything.

T: OK, now label everything in this room that you don't like.

C: OK. I don't like the pictures. They are cheap. I don't really like this table. It is also cheap. The wall colors are only OK.

T: Awesome. My guess is that you could keep going. I don't really need you to do that. I just wanted to you to see that your mind can name just about everything. It can also evaluate just about everything. We don't even need to try to do this. It just occurs. It's natural.

After the client understands that, ask the client about times when their mind does this same thing and it brings their life down. For example, how does the mind treat thoughts about the client's life and successes? What does the mind say about feelings that occur when asking someone out on a date? We are not saying the mind has nothing useful to say—simply that it has an opinion about everything and that this limits our ability to interact with things nonjudgmentally.

T: Humor me for just a minute. What if every parent taught their child to see anxiety for what it is: a physiological response? This is sort of a magical question because society, media, and loved ones will all teach the child anxiety is "bad." But what if a child could experience anxiety without any language added to it and be given the freedom to see what they naturally and honestly think about anxiety? As someone who has been working at this for a long time, I can tell you, having an open mind allows you to see these events differently. I am more flexible with anxiety now than I was before, and that comes from seeing it for what it is not what it says it is. It is not our job to stop the cognitive process; we could not do this even if we tried. And we probably have tried. Our job is to learn what to do with it when it happens. There are many ways to think about our minds. I like to think of it as an announcer at a sporting event, a child in a kindergarten class, or a salesperson who is trying to convince you to purchase something. They may say useful things every once in a while, but a lot of what they say is not helpful and sometimes even harmful if acted on. Let's try an exercise right now to see what it might be like to do something different with your thoughts. Simply notice them as thoughts without getting caught up in them, fighting with them, or believing everything they say is true.

There are a number of exercises you can use in the moment to help your clients practice defusion. We list a few in the sections that follow, but we recommend picking one and sticking with it to help your clients really get defusion, rather than running through several exercises superficially. You can use the other exercises at a different time. A good strategy is to have the client practice it in session with you, debrief to help ensure the exercise has a defusion function, troubleshoot any issues, and then assign it for homework.

Objective versus subjective evaluations

A brief exercise you could use at this point would be to expand on a discussion of how our minds add evaluations and judgments to experiences. We like to help clients see that our thoughts will offer objective evaluations of things at times and subjective evaluations at other times. Both can be useful depending on context; subjective evaluations can sometimes cloud an event. For example, a "long test" is different from an "unfairly long test." Adding that subjective part can alter the experience of that test. While there is no stopping these mostly automatic evaluations, it is worth helping the client be aware that this occurs. We like to teach this by using a common item, such as a water bottle.

> T: I'd like to do a little exercise with you to help us see the funny things our minds do. Let me find something in this room that is fairly common. OK, here is the water bottle I have been drinking out of today. I'd like you to tell me objective things about this bottle. Tell me things everyone would agree with.
>
> C: OK, it's a cycling type water bottle—one a person riding a bicycle would use. It's clear with a black cap. It has an "S" on the side. It's smaller than other types of cycling water bottles. It's pretty scratched up. If I held it without water, it would be light.
>
> T: Awesome. Now tell me subjective things. Things not everyone might say.
>
> C: It's too small. Thus, it is not a good one because the bigger ones hold more water. It is a cheap one. It's the type of bottle you get for free at some event. It's old because it is all scratched up. Also, it's not neat, new, and pretty like other ones. I don't really like it. It looks like it would leak.
>
> T: That is great. Thanks so much. Now let's do the same thing with the feeling of anxiety. Give me objective descriptions about anxiety. What are elements of your anxiety that are facts, things everyone would agree with?
>
> C: OK. It involves thoughts about how I don't fit in. My heart goes faster. My muscles tighten up. My stomach feels different.
>
> T: Now tell me about the subjective part.
>
> C: I hate it! I wish I was different. I think it is unfair. It hurts. It sucks!
>
> T: Thanks. Doing this exercise is not really an answer to your anxiety. But it can be useful to see the difference in the factual parts of anxiety—thoughts, muscle tension, stomach discomfort—and its subjective parts—hate, unfairness, pain. One part is inherent to anxiety. The other part we are adding. Let's practice focusing on the objective part over the next week. When you have a difficult experience, see if you can notice the objective parts and also the subjective parts your mind adds to it. Just watch your mind at work as it adds evaluations and judgments. Notice what happens to the power of these evaluations and judgments when you practice watching your mind.

Labeling-thoughts mindfulness exercise

This is a common mindfulness exercise in which clients practice attending to their breath, noticing when their attention wanders to thoughts, simply labeling the thought as "thinking," and returning back to the breath when ready. Labeling thoughts for what they are, rather than focusing on their content, is a way to practice defusion. This exercise is grounded with the attentional focus on the breath. This way, clients can notice when they lose their focus (as they focus on thoughts instead of breathing) and have something to attend to after defusing from a thought. We recommend guiding your client through the meditation for 5 minutes or so, giving enough time and pauses between your prompts to experience what it is like to get lost in thoughts, catch and label the process, and return to the breath.

We typically introduce the exercise with something like this:

> Let's try something to help you practice noticing when you get stuck in your thoughts and how to get unstuck. For the next few minutes I'm going to ask you to close your eyes and attend to your breath. As you focus on the sensations of breathing in and out, your attention will naturally wander to other things, including thoughts. The core of this practice will be to notice when you are caught up in your thoughts and label them by repeating gently in your head "thinking." In other words, rather than focusing on what your thoughts are saying, just acknowledge them as part of the natural process of thinking. After you label "thinking" a few times in your mind, gently return your focus back to your breath. You might find some thoughts are strong and your attention doesn't wander back quickly or that you get caught up in new thoughts just a moment later. Whatever you experience is totally fine, the important thing is to stick with noticing your thoughts and labeling them as "thinking" even if you spend the whole exercise doing so.

We would then guide the client through the mindfulness exercise. We typically ask clients to get in a comfortable and alert position with both feet firmly on the ground and their eyes closed or gaze focused a few feet in front of them. We recommend memorizing some common prompts for guiding the exercise but not reading a script, so it flows more naturally and so you can practice at the same time with your client (after all, it can be helpful for therapists too).

Here is an outline for a labeling mindfulness exercise you can generally follow. Keep in mind the pauses between prompts are key, so your clients have time to practice what they've been instructed. We typically recommend having more frequent prompts at the start and spacing them out more and more as the client gets going in the exercise.

1. Get centered: Take a few moments to get present. Notice the sounds you can hear right now . . . the sensation of your feet contacting the floor . . . of your body contacting the chair . . . .

2. Focus on the breath: Now bring all of your attention to your breathing. . . . Following the sensations of your breath as you inhale . . . and exhale. . . .

3. Notice when your attention wanders: When your attention wanders, as it will naturally do, simply acknowledge whatever caught your attention. If it's a thought, just label it "thinking" in your mind. . . . And then return back to the breath when you are ready.

4. Encourage ongoing labeling: Continue to focus on your breath. . . noticing and labeling your thoughts as "thinking." . . . Each time you get caught up in thoughts, just repeat "thinking" in your mind. . . . Practice labeling for a few more breaths. . . .

5. Expand awareness: Take a few moments to expand your awareness . . . noticing the sensations of your feet contacting the floor . . . the sounds in the room . . . and when you are ready, open your eyes.

After the exercise, debrief with the client, focusing on what their experience was like practicing the exercise. While there are many things that a client could take away from an exercise like this, hopefully your setup and the manner in which you presented it orients the client to notice how they get caught in their thoughts. You may note to clients that we all get caught up in thoughts, and a primary purpose of the practice is to simply practice catching when this happens. It is also worth helping clients notice how they can let go of thoughts they get caught up in and return to just labeling them for what they are. We suggest telling the client that this can be a useful exercise to practice as it will allow them to notice their thinking and give them a pause so they can decide whether to listen to their thinking or not.

Breaking the rules

This last exercise focuses on guiding your client to set a behavioral commitment related to defusion. This involves helping your client identify a "rule" their mind gives them that is unhelpful to follow, a way they could act inconsistently with the rule, and a commitment to break the rule, with a specific goal.

You can introduce the exercise with something like this:

Our minds give us many rules it says we should live by. Rules can be great at times, helping us stick to our goals, do what is effective, and stay out of trouble. For example, my rule "brush your teeth every night" helps me keep my teeth clean even when I don't feel like it, or "treat other people the way I want to be treated" helps me be caring to other people even when I have the urge to snap at them. Unfortunately, we usually leave our minds in charge when deciding what rules to follow, and not all rules are helpful. For example, my rule "meet your commitments" seems helpful, but I notice that it also leads me to overprioritize work over other important things in my life, or burning out on work rather than asking for an extension. What is a rule your mind gives you that isn't helpful?

You could then work with the client to identify a rule they get fused with and that leads to unhelpful actions, which might be relevant to work on for the next week. If your client has trouble identifying one, you might recall previous discussions you've had with them or work backward from a problem situation they reported. If you really struggle with finding a personally relevant rule, you could also help them identify a more common, unhelpful rule (e.g., "finish your plate") or even a reasonable rule that they could still practice breaking (e.g., "shower before leaving the house"). Part of the function of this homework is to introduce flexible responding to a rule. That is, you want to teach your client that rules can be broken sometimes.

Once you've identified an unhelpful rule, you can introduce the idea of breaking it.

Looking back on this rule, you probably feel pretty sure it isn't always useful. But in the moment, your mind is persuasive and convinces you to follow it. What we need to do is start practicing and strengthening your ability to break these rules by doing things that go against the rule. Just like with practicing playing a musical instrument, the more you work on breaking your rules, the better you will be at it and the more likely you can do it well when it matters. This can feel very uncomfortable and your mind won't like it. That's good if you notice discomfort because it means it will help strengthen your rule-breaking skills—just like how a hard bike ride means you are strengthening your biking muscles. So, what could you do this week that would break your rule?

Once you've identified a specific behavior that would be inconsistent with the rule, take a few moments to strengthen the commitment. Make sure the commitment is specific (i.e., stating what the client will do, when, for how long), is realistic, and refers to an observable action (something another person can confirm they did). Also, get a feel for whether the client is committed, and if not, explore how to modify the goal or otherwise enhance commitment.

HOW DO WE KNOW WHICH INNER EXPERIENCES TO LISTEN TO?

We do not generally hear this concern from clients, but we often hear this from people we train. Trainees sometimes worry if a client successfully practices defusion, they might stop listening to any thoughts they have and behave as if they were no longer guided by a conscience. We understand where that fear comes from. We just explained the benefits of and problems with having cognition. The way we usually address this is by reminding the client that cognitions are helpful when the client can objectively say they are helpful. They are not helpful when they take the client away from what they want in life. The client will need to adopt this new way of evaluating cognitions. We would explain it like this:

> Sometimes, clients worry about how they will know which thoughts to listen to. I like to think of it like this: All thoughts are suggestions. Some are useful and some are not. You will have to practice and see what works for you. But you will need to be honest with yourself about this. I think following some thoughts will not improve your life, whereas following other thoughts may. Until you actually follow through on behaviors, you may not be able to tell which thoughts are helpful to listen to. It can be a funny thing. I have had some of the most fun times in my life at events I did not want to go to. I have had some of the best outcomes when I chose to approach while my inner experiences were telling me to stay away. Over time, I have come to learn how things work for me. I'm not perfect at it, but I have been surprised by the odd signals my mind sends me. It certainly tells me things but sometimes they are cryptic, and I get to figure out how much power I want them to have over my actions.

WRAP UP WITH HOMEWORK

We recommend setting a behavioral commitment every session, so your client always has something to work on or at least think about in between sessions. The objective is to create opportunities for generalization of skills to real-life situations and extend your influence on your client's life as much as possible. Remember that what you are teaching in session may not be automatically reinforced in your client's environment, so you will need to provide some scaffolding to increase the likelihood your client contacts natural reinforcers (e.g., by engaging in meaningful action). Given that this session focused on acceptance and defusion, ask your client to identify a behavioral commitment that will allow them to practice these skills. We recommend extending the exercise practiced in session (e.g., noticing objective versus subjective thoughts, brief mindfulness practice, or breaking an unhelpful rule) so your client has the opportunity to "get" defusion. If appropriate, you could also assign a more general homework task:

T: What is a situation in which you would really want to be able to practice willingness and noticing thoughts as thoughts?

C: Probably when I'm trying to text my friends to hang out with me. I never end up doing it because I feel like a burden and that everyone hates me.

T: That's a great example. Those sound like powerful thoughts right now.

C: Yeah. They feel that way.

T: Why would it be important to you to text these friends?

c: Because I want to have friends and I like being around people. I like connecting with others. I don't want to be a hermit.

T: OK. How many times would you like to text your friends to hang out this week?

c: Maybe let's start with one time.

T: Great, and what specifically would you need to practice to send the text?

c: Well, I would need to let the fear of rejection just be there . . . and I would need to notice those self-critical thoughts as thoughts. And I guess I would need to just send the stupid text anyway.

T: All that sounds great. What external barriers might get in the way of your meeting this goal?

c: Nothing, really. It'll take me less than a minute so I will have time. It's more the internal stuff that will make this hard.

T: And what might make it easier for you to meet this commitment?

c: Telling you about it now and knowing we are going to talk about it next week will probably help.

T: OK, and I will be sure to check in with you next week.

After this conversation (or during it if your client is all right with that), complete the *Behavioral Commitment Worksheet* provided in Appendix C in this book. Make sure your client agrees with and relates to the words written down in the worksheet. The function of the worksheet is to bring some of the therapeutic context outside the therapy room to facilitate generalization of skills. It is not just another checklist to be completed.

SESSION SUMMARY

By the end of these sessions, your client should have learned the basics of acceptance and defusion. Throughout these sessions you have walked your client through exercises, metaphors, and discussions about emotions and real-life events to understand what it is like to relate to inner experiences in an accepting and defused way. Your clients should have an understanding of why this new way of relating to their thoughts and feelings matters to them and fits with their goals for therapy. You have also assigned behavioral commitments for homework in the past few sessions to support your clients' practice of acceptance and defusion, so they can apply these skills to meaningful life activities and goals.

7

Sessions 5 and 6

Acceptance, Defusion, Mindfulness, and Values

You should be at your fifth therapy session—depending on how quickly your client grasped the concepts covered in previous chapters. By now, your client should see their clinical issue a little differently. Hopefully, they no longer work to control specific thoughts, feelings, or emotions and now work to respond to them in more useful ways. They should also be orienting their actions toward living a meaningful life rather than regulating emotions. In this session, you will review and continue to build on skills your client has already been working on while incorporating new processes of change. By helping your client see how all the processes of change are connected, you might shift how they practice these skills and move them toward doing so more effectively.

REVIEW HOMEWORK

At the start of every session from now on, you will spend the first few minutes reviewing the behavioral commitment you set with your client last week. As we mentioned in the previous chapter, you will want to go over a couple key points with your client: (1) "What was it like to do things you care about?" and (2) "Psychologically (or internally), what was it like to try and make these changes?" The objective in reviewing homework is to guide your client toward contacting their direct experience of trying out new behaviors so they can judge—on the basis of their values—whether those behaviors worked for them. As you talk about the homework, you should also be assessing areas of skills deficits and emphasize them accordingly in your session.

REVIEW PURPOSE OF THERAPY: VALUES

The concept of values gets addressed later in this book, but it can often be useful to give a taste of the concept earlier in treatment. It is nice to talk about values after acceptance and defusion have been addressed. Without acceptance and defusion, a discussion about values can be somewhat rule-bound and less meaningful. For example, if someone is avoidant of feeling strong emotion and their thoughts are perceived as powerful, they may be unwilling to experience the internal events that go along with stating values inconsistent with their actions. For example, if someone really valued time with family but was so busy with work that they were not home at night or during the weekends, stating that to a therapist would likely evoke a feeling of guilt or sadness. Practicing a little acceptance and defusion lessens the blow of stating one's genuine values.

There are times when a prolonged discussion of values earlier in therapy is wise. In our experience, it is worthwhile to spend a bit of time on values earlier in therapy, when motivation to change behavior is low. We have found motivation is generally high for behavior change with certain disorders such as anxiety disorders. Individuals who present with disorders that are egosyntonic (i.e., enjoyable), such as trichotillomania, substance use, and eating disorders, would particularly benefit from discussing how life might be better with some behavior change. Additionally, some clients might just benefit from having a little extra meaning to the therapy. Because acceptance and defusion have only been touched on at this point, it makes sense to have just a brief discussion about values to give meaning to therapy and provide better direction.

One of the things that has always struck us about our clients is the enormous amount of time they have spent trying to regulate internal experiences. In contrast, people we know who are functioning pretty well maybe spend 10% of their day regulating their internal experiences. This is because instead of expending time and energy attempting to control internal experiences, they spend time on things meaningful to them. This is a simple explanation of what we are hoping to help our clients accomplish: decrease the amount of time spent trying to regulate internal experiences and increase the amount of time spent pursuing valued activities.

Presenting this conceptualization to a client can orient them to the rewards of pursuing values and some of the pitfalls of attempting to regulate internal experiences. The following conversation exemplifies this.

> THERAPIST (T): We have been working together for a handful of sessions and it seems like we are making progress. There is one issue I would like to spend a few minutes on. In many ways, I think we should have gone over this earlier in therapy, but I also don't know if it makes as much sense at that point. Are you open to going over a new topic?
>
> CLIENT (C): Yes, and I'm curious.
>
> T: What do you think is the point of our work together?

c: I originally thought it was going to be learning how to control my anxiety, but I've come to believe it is more about learning how to handle it when it shows up.

T: OK. But why would you want to control it or learn how to handle it better?

c: I guess so I can get back into life.

T: Yes, that is sort of what I was thinking, too. My guess is that we are working together so you can have all the exciting parts of your life back, but because anxiety is such a roadblock right now, we spend the whole time talking about anxiety, your relationship to it, and how you respond to it. It makes it seem like therapy is about anxiety when we wouldn't even be talking about it unless it was getting in the way of your doing what is important to you.

c: That's a good point. We really have been focusing on it. But we do talk about how my life is going in general.

T: Yes, we do. But let's spend just a few moments on the big picture of why we are doing this. Prior to coming in to work with me, what percent of each day was spent trying to regulate your anxiety?

c: It's hard to say, because sometimes it was for a few seconds every minute. There were other times when it was hours on end. But if I was awake for 16 hours a day—sometimes more when I was awake and worrying—I would say at least half of each day was spent caught up in my anxiety in some way. Wow, that is depressing!

T: It's what it is. I always think it is positive that you are seeing this, so you can choose to handle it differently. OK, but back to the 50% of your day spent regulating anxiety. Where do you think you are now, after a month of us working together?

c: Maybe 40%. At least I recognize it and try to do things differently.

T: OK, great. Have you found your life is improving or our work is making it less desirable?

c: Improving.

T: OK, so it is worth moving forward with this type of work. I'd like for us to think about our work as taking time from control and moving it to living. There is only so much time in your day. As you decrease the amount of time spent regulating emotions, what would you like to spend that time on?

c: What do you mean?

T: Let's say you open up an hour of time and energy per day. I think you should fill that with meaningful things. I'd like to discuss what those things are for you. For example, some days when I get in to work I tell myself, "If you don't putter on the internet, you can leave an hour early today." I'm swapping my putter/procrastination time for something more interesting.

c: OK, I would love to cook more, exercise, garden, call family, generally keep up with the house, stuff like that.

T: Awesome. So, one of the things I would really like to see this week is increasing time spent each day on something you enjoy but that you would not have done previously. That is, I'd like to see an increase in pleasurable or meaningful activities each day. Instead of adding a whole hour per day, how about we just add one thing? I don't care how long it takes, but I'd like you to do one thing you find meaningful that you have not been doing as much as you'd like to every day.

C: OK, I think I get it. Each day I need to do something new and meaningful?

T: Yes, just do one little thing. Maybe it is going to the gym, cooking dinner, seeing a friend, calling home, whatever.

C: OK.

T: And one last thing, let's be flexible. Sometimes the thing you plan will not work. A client will plan on calling mom or dad, and then call and they were not home. If that happens, do something else. Go for a walk. Call a sibling or a friend. Try a new food. Do something.

C: OK.

REVIEW ACCEPTANCE AND OFFER EXERCISES

This is a good opportunity to go over acceptance with a real-life example. The method described here was also explained in Chapter 6. Ask the client about a situation in which they struggled with implementing acceptance. We like to say something like, "Tell me about a situation where you wanted to practice acceptance but found it difficult." When the client describes a situation where they struggled, it is your job to keep asking questions about that situation so that they can start to get a sense of what it really felt like. You want them to start to experience that event—as if it were happening in the session. You might ask:

- What thoughts did you have in that situation?
- How did you respond to that feeling?
- Do you feel you often struggle in situations like this?
- How do you wish you had handled that situation?

Your goal is to have a conversation about the situation to help the client experience some of the internal experiences that came along with that event. As the feeling from that event starts to be more present in the room, you can work with the client to practice acceptance. It might look something like this:

T: Tell me about a situation where you wanted to practice willingness and ran into difficulty.

C: I was with my kids and they were driving me nuts. I just asked them to help set the table for dinner and they were not helpful at all. They would do one step and then disappear. So, I'd call them back and ask them to finish the job, and they would add one more thing to the table before disappearing again. Finally, I yelled at them. I really don't want to yell. But after asking them like five times to do one simple thing, I lost it. If I can vent for a second, I cook a whole healthy meal and clean up all the pots and pans. I also do the shopping and meal planning. I just want this little bit of help and they won't even do that!

T: What thoughts were you having?

C: I was pissed off. I kept thinking this was not fair. I had thoughts about how this type of thing happens to me all the time. I was thinking about how my family takes me for granted. (Note: In this example, the client is already feeling some of the emotions from that event. If the client is not in touch with the emotions from that event, we suggest digging at this some more. Usually, after talking about an emotional situation, the person begins to feel some of the associated emotions.)

T: Are you willing to work on something with me?

C: Sure.

T: I'd like you to notice what you are feeling right now. Please describe what is occurring within you in this moment.

C: I'm feeling angry. I'm picturing the dinner. I'm replaying past situations that were like it. Even though the event was a few days ago, I am experiencing aspects of it.

T: Let's talk about how you are treating those thoughts and feelings. Right now, are you open to them and giving them space, or are you struggling against them?

C: That's funny you ask. Because I know what I am supposed to be doing, but I somehow let my guard down in this room. I was totally caught up in the thoughts. I wasn't fighting them because there is no danger of them right now, but I was definitely giving them a lot of attention. They pulled me out of the moment.

T: OK. Thanks for being honest. I'd like us to do a little practice where we work on just noticing what our minds are giving us and not getting entangled with them. Retell the story about what happened in the kitchen, I will continue to ask you questions about it, but when you tell me, I want you to also objectively state what is happening inside your body. For example, I am having the thought that . . . , or I am experiencing the feeling of . . . , or I am experiencing tightness in my . . . . Pretend you are an announcer of your body and you just tell me what is happening. This will help you be more aware of what is going on inside you and also give you a little separation from those thoughts and feelings.

We are not going to write out this whole conversation, but hopefully the conversation moves forward and the client has some practice experiencing their internal experiences in a more open and defused fashion.

Here are some example strategies you could use after having a conversation about a time when the client struggled with an inner experience. We would recommend just picking one to focus on in a session to extend practicing acceptance.

Self-compassion

This is a simple exercise to help clients practice being compassionate toward themselves and their experiences:

> Take a moment to picture a vulnerable person or animal that you would want to automatically take care of, like a scared puppy, a crying child, or a hurt friend. What comes to mind? Now picture this child [or whatever they picked] was feeling hurt [or whatever emotion you are working with]. What would you want to say to them? How would you want to treat them? What if you treated yourself and your pain in the same way?

Flexible attention with a painful emotion

One way to guide your clients in practicing acceptance in the moment is to give them a variety of prompts and questions to direct them to flexibly interact with a painful current emotion. The idea is to have your client approach the emotion and remain in contact with it while acknowledging the emotion for what it is. Really, anything works that approaches the emotion without wallowing in, giving into, or fighting with it. You might cover these within a mindful conversation you have back and forth with the client or in a more eyes-closed exercise in which you guide the client. We provide here a list of example prompts you can use. Pick as few or as many as fits the situation.

- Acknowledging: "Take a moment to acknowledge whatever emotion you are experiencing right now. Put it into words by describing what you are feeling—like, 'I'm feeling anxious right now.'"
- Observing physical sensations: "Where do you feel this emotion in your body? Take a few moments to notice the sensations and what they feel like in your body."
- Breathing: "Picture breathing into this emotion and where you feel it in your body. With each breath, open up to and make space for what you are feeling."
- Watching how it changes: "Continue to watch the emotion and notice how the experience changes over time. Does it get more or less intense over time or sort of cycle up and down? Does it expand or contract? How does it move in your body?"
- Prompting acceptance with a metaphor, such as: "Welcome it like you might welcome an old friend," "Appreciate it like you might appreciate a

beautiful sunset," "Hold it lightly like you might hold a delicate flower," or "Inspect it with curiosity, noticing the subtle details, like you might look at a work of art."

- Listening to it: "Our emotions are often telling us something. It could be about something important, things that need to be changed, our current situation, and so on. What is your emotion telling you?"

Changing *but* into *and*

Experiential avoidance shows up in the reasons clients give for not doing things that matter to them (e.g., "I want to get out of the house more but I'm too tired," "I want to quit smoking but I can't handle the withdrawal symptoms," "I would talk to them about this but I'm scared they will get upset"). These statements give the illusion that difficult thoughts and feelings are truly preventing clients from doing what matters, suggesting avoidance is the only possible solution. You can explain this idea to your client and help them identify their own *but* statement. If your client struggles to articulate their *but* statement, you can provide sentence stems for them to complete, based on what you know about their history. For example, "I really want to stop checking my locks, but." Be sure to use an overt behavior in the sentence stem because your client can actually control what they do—not necessarily what they think or feel.

Next, introduce the idea of changing the *but* into an *and*. You can say something like this:

What if instead of a *but* you used an *and*? For example, "I want to get out of the house more and I'm tired." We are still acknowledging that you're very tired, and being tired does not negate your desire to get out of the house or stop you from actually getting out of the house. You can get out of the house *and* feel very tired, just like how you probably have gotten out of bed before when you felt like you couldn't get up. Your inner experiences can come along for the ride and they don't have to stop you from doing what matters. It's not so much about the change in language. You don't have to convince yourself you aren't tired. Rather, what if you changed your stance toward your inner world using an *and* approach? That means you choose what you want to do *and* make room for whatever difficult thoughts and feelings show up.

This exercise can help set up a behavioral commitment for the week or even a way to practice acceptance in the moment during the session. Within this framework you can help your client identify something they want to do while having a challenging inner experience. Then, you can help them set a goal where they do what matters *and* open up to the difficult thoughts and feelings that might arise.

REVIEW DEFUSION AND OFFER EXERCISES

Defusion is about seeing internal events for what they really are—events that occur within one's body. It can be a thought like, "This will never work out for me," a feeling like withdrawal symptoms for someone struggling with some type of dependence, or a physiological sensation, such as chest pain in a panic attack. These are all important experiences that tell the client something is going on. Given our cognitive abilities, we usually experience the thought, feeling, or sensation as much more than it really is. For example, we experience a memory about a negatively evaluated event as distressing even though it is a memory about an event and not the actual event. Defusion exercises help the client see their internal experiences as what they actually are: thoughts, feelings, or bodily sensations about events, rather than the actual events.

As learning how to be experiential with exercises is key to doing ACT well, we are going to use the same strategy we used for acceptance with defusion: Have a conversation about a time when the client was fused with thoughts, stay on that topic long enough that some of the experiences of fusion start to show up, and then conclude with some work on defusion, like an exercise or an appropriate discussion. If you can get good at this skill, you will likely be successful at implementing ACT across many situations and clinical presentations. The following dialogue should give you an idea of how this would work.

T: Tell me about a thought, feeling, or sensation that really pulled you in over this last week.

C: Do you mean in a good or bad way?

T: If you are asking whether it pulled you in a way that is consistent with your values or not, yes, that is what I am getting at. I believe we get to choose when to listen to our internal experiences. Sometimes things work out well when we listen to these inner experiences, and sometimes they don't. Give me an example of when getting caught up in or listening to your internal experiences turned out poorly.

C: I had one that really stood out. I was doing homework with my child— which is just frustrating on its own. I had also just read a frustrating work e-mail before that so I was feeling more uptight than usual. My son needed to read aloud for 20 minutes. It's not really that big a deal because we alternate pages so he's only reading for maybe 15 of the minutes, plus we are hanging out, which he enjoys. Then, he starts whining about how he doesn't want to read, can he just do it later, and all this stuff. I'm being calm and helpful and working with him through it. Eventually, we are 10 minutes in, no pages have been read, and he's on the floor whining and crying. It's all just bubbling up inside me. I'm thinking things like, "You'd be half way done if you just started when I got into your room" and "He should not be allowed to act this way!" So, that is all building up and then I yell, "Knock it off!" He immediately stops and has that deer-in-the-headlights look. I don't think I've yelled at him in years. Of course, I feel like total crap now.

T: That's rough.

C: Yes, it is. Then my wife comes in and gives me a supportive look, like she gets it and knows how bad I feel. I think she says something like, "I've got his one," and she takes over with the kid. I say, "I'm sorry," and leave. I go back later in the evening and talk about it with him. But of course, I just wish it never happened.

T: There are lots of rough parts to that, but I'd like to focus on how you were interacting with what was going on inside of you as your child was misbehaving. Tell me more about what you were thinking.

C: Oh, it was a continuous stream of, "This is obnoxious," "This is why you struggle at reading," "You'd be pretty far along if you just started sooner," "I don't want to reinforce this type of behavior," and so on.

T: It sounds like lots of judgments about the situation and his actions. How were you experiencing those thoughts?

C: That's a good question. They were overwhelming. They were huge. I was totally caught up in them. As we're talking about it, I can tell that was not helpful.

T: Did you have any separation from those thoughts?

C: None. I was totally wrapped up in them.

T: How do you feel about that moment?

C: Embarrassed. Depressed. I wish I could take it back.

T: How are you feeling right now?

C: Depressed and embarrassed. I can also give myself a little space because I know parenting is difficult. I am good at parenting most of the time. But I still have shivers when I think about yelling at my kid just because he won't read. I mean, everything I know about parenting says to find a new way to do homework. You know, get some rewards, make it a little easier, make it more fun.

T: OK, can you feel the struggle here?

C: Yes, I'm feeling pretty frustrated and keep replaying the event in my mind.

T: OK, I'd like you to hold on to that thought or feeling. Really stay with it. Don't push it away. I'd like to do an exercise with it.

Seeing thoughts more concretely

In this exercise, pick an object in the room and interact with it as if it was your client's thoughts, exploring more and less helpful ways of responding to the thought. This can help make abstract concepts more concrete and give you a shorthand you can refer back to in later conversations. The specific object is unimportant. We often use a piece of paper, clipboard, or other large object that can block one's view when held close to the face, for ease of teaching. You can also write the thought on a card.

T: Suppose this paper was the thought, "This is obnoxious," and other thoughts that came up with your child. It sounds like you got really stuck in the thought when it came up last night. If this paper was the thought, how were you responding to it?

C: I don't know. . . . I guess I was pretty caught up with it.

T: OK, so it was like the thought was right in front of your face with all of your attention going to it. [Hold the piece of paper close to your own face.] What can I see right now when this thought is up in my face?

C: Not much. The paper is blocking you.

T: Yes, and my focus is on the thought—not you, our conversation, or any other thing I could be focusing on and doing. It's pretty hard to interact with people when we are so caught up in our thoughts. What else could you do with this thought [pointing to the piece of paper]?

C: I could throw it away.

T: Yes, that's often what we think to do. I don't like my thoughts so I'll get rid of them. This would be like trying to argue with the thought [shake the piece of paper while staring at it] or maybe trying to push the thought away [hold the paper away with a straight arm and out of sight]. Now the thought isn't in my face, but notice my focus and effort is on keeping this thought away. My arm is going to get sore eventually. And what happens eventually with these thoughts?

C: They come back.

T: Yes, and I'm right back to arguing or getting stuck in them. Well, the strategies we've been talking about in therapy might give us a different way of responding to these thoughts. What if I just acknowledged the thought for what it was, allowed it to be there, and then got on with life [put the thought in your lap]? Importantly, I'm not fighting with or trying to ignore the thought. It's right there in my lap and I can see it out of the corner of my eye. When the thought is in my lap, what can I focus on?

C: I guess whatever we are talking about?

T: That's right. Now, my attention and energy are open and available to focus on whatever I want to be doing right now. Sure, the thought might creep back up [bring thought up to the face], but I can notice it once again as just a thought and return to what we were doing. With this in mind, here's a question for you. If you were going to put your thoughts in your lap, what might you do right now? Or how could I tell right now if you were just letting your thoughts be there in your lap?

C: Hmmm . . . I don't really know.

T: Well, for example, for me, I'm noticing a thought, "I have to explain it better." If I get caught up in the thought [hold paper to face] I could talk all day, explaining away the concepts and ideas. If I put the thought in my lap, then I return to our conversation and what I want to be doing right now, which is being curious about your experience and supporting you in making meaningful changes in your life. I'd ask you more questions rather than explain things to you. And there I go right now explaining away. What about for you? How could I tell if you are placing your thoughts in your lap?

From there, help the client identify something they could do in session to practice defusion. You might need to help them notice a thought they are stuck with if one has not been identified and what they are pulled to do when they get stuck in the thought. Ultimately, fusion is about how thoughts affect our actions, so this exercise can help make sure we get to defusion in terms of doing something different that is less dominated by our thoughts. Often, this looks like doing what would be meaningful or effective in the moment that the client might otherwise do if they were less stuck in or fused to a thought. That said, you could also use this exercise to explain defusion without the in-session behavioral commitment and instead assign homework based on this exercise. Once you've worked through this exercise, you can use it as a brief reminder when discussing fused and defused responses to thoughts in future sessions (e.g., bringing the paper up close to your face when you notice your client being fused, or returning to the question of what they might do if they put the thought back in their lap).

MINDFULNESS OR FLEXIBLE ATTENTION

After you have reviewed acceptance and defusion, teach flexible attention. Being able to pay close attention to what is important is helpful for all clients. Some clinical presentations call for it more than others, but it is useful for everyone. Sometimes we call it "being present" because our clients are usually caught up in their internal events and do a poor job at being present: They ruminate on the past or worry about the future. But accurately speaking, the most useful thing we can learn is how to pay attention to what is most useful for us at any given moment and how to shift our attention depending on the situation. For example, if I (M.P.T.) am working on this book, most of my focus should be here, but I should also be able to adjust that focus if needed. Similarly, if a client who struggles with anxiety begins to experience high anxiety during some important event, it is fine if the anxiety is noticed, but we would also want the client to be able to focus on other important stimuli, such as the primary task in which they were engaging.

This allows the client to notice something and quickly decide whether to pay attention to that or focus their attention elsewhere. Most of us do not consciously decide what to pay attention to. We simply move along with our lives and pay attention to things that work for us. But for many people, we can benefit from learning when we are about to be pulled into something that is not useful for us and intentionally put our attention elsewhere.

Thus, we like to present flexible attention training—or mindfulness—as choosing what to pay attention to in any given moment, based on one's values.

It is important to explain this to your client, as many will believe the purpose of the "mindfulness" activity is about relaxation or not being affected by stressors. To us, it is more about noticing that stressors will try and grab you and choosing how much attention you are going to give them. Please explain that to the client. This is also one of the more formal exercises we will do in this therapy. Give the client a solid rationale for the exercise, practice it once in session, and then ask the client to practice it every day until the next session. You will also want to contextualize the work so they can generalize skills gained from the exercise to other situations. We do not want mindfulness exercises to only be used when practicing mindfulness.

The following dialogue is a common way to present a mindfulness exercise from an ACT perspective.

T: At all times, we are paying attention to something. Maybe some of us can pay close attention to a handful of things at the same time, but generally, we focus on just a few important things. For example, I am paying attention to you, how you are doing right now, and whether we are addressing the important issues we should address. I am also paying a little attention to the time and small things like that. Other thoughts are coming in, like other projects I have to get done, and maybe that I am feeling a little hungry or thirsty or even have to go to the bathroom. But I am choosing to let those thoughts go. I'd like to do an exercise aimed at helping you notice times your mind tries to pull you away from whatever you have going on. Is this OK with you?

C: Yes, sure.

T: This will last about 10 minutes. I'd like you to either close your eyes or, if you prefer, stare at a spot that is not distracting, such as the floor or wall. The point of this exercise is to help you see the difference between observing your thoughts and buying into your thoughts. At points during this exercise, you will be watching your thoughts and be very aware this exercise is occurring. Then, there will be other times when you find yourself caught up in a thought. For me, I go for about a minute observing what I am thinking before I have the thought some deadline is approaching and I get caught up in how and when I am going to get the project done. Those are moments when I buy into my thoughts. The exercise stops and I am just there thinking about the project.

I'll walk you through this exercise. I'd like you to practice noticing your thoughts, and recognize when you get caught up in one. You will know that because the whole exercise will stop and you will just be thinking about that thing. When that happens, recognize that it occurred, and get back into the exercise.

WE HAVE ONE MAIN GOAL HERE: We are recognizing thoughts as thoughts as they occur and noticing when we get grabbed by a thought. We are not trying to push any thoughts away or have more or less of certain thoughts. We are not concerned with whether doing this exercise causes

you to feel more relaxed or more stressed. You will feel how you feel
during this exercise. What questions do you have?

C: None.

T: Then, like I said, either close your eyes or stare at a blank space where
you won't be distracted. Also, sit comfortably so you won't have to adjust
much over the next 10 minutes. Pretend you are looking at a large screen.
It can be a movie screen, a stage, an outdoor screen, whatever works for
you. Put whatever comes to your mind next up on that screen. We are
not pushing it away or trying to get rid of anything; we are just watching
what shows up.

I don't need you to talk to me at all during this exercise. Just follow
along with what I say. Just sit there and observe what your mind gives
you. Notice what occurs. It might be a thought, a picture, maybe even a
feeling. Whatever occurs, I'd like you to put on the screen what you are
picturing in your mind. Then, once it is on the screen, I'd just like you
to notice it is there. Just observe it. Our job is to simply observe that
thought, nothing else.

If you are having the thought, "I am not sure what he means," then put
that thought up on the screen and observe it. If you think, "This is
stupid," just observe that thought, too. Whatever comes to your mind,
just watch it.

There will come a point when you are not observing the thought and
you are caught up in it. You will be thinking about that thought. There
is nothing wrong with that. I just want you to recognize that it occurred
and go back to watching your thoughts.

I am going to stop talking for a couple minutes so you can focus on the
exercise. Please watch your thoughts for the next few minutes and pay
attention to times when you are pulled into your thoughts. [Wait a few
minutes.]

OK, please continue with the exercise. I hope you had the experience of
watching your thoughts and being caught up in them. Again, I'll give
you a few more minutes to observe what occurs in your head. Put your
thoughts up on the screen and wait for the next one to show up. If the
same types of thoughts keep showing up, that is fine. Just put those
thoughts up on the screen. At some point, you will likely lose the exercise
and be thinking about one of your thoughts. [Again, give the client a few
minutes to notice the thoughts that are occurring.]

Good work. Go ahead and picture what the room looks like. Open your
eyes. Tell me what you noticed in that exercise.

C: I will admit I was a little confused initially. But as we got going, the exercise made sense. I was able to watch my thinking for parts of the exercise.

T: Did you also have those moments when you were caught up in the
thoughts and the exercise stopped?

C: Yes, a couple times. It usually occurred around something I found important. It was easy to just notice thoughts about being tired or hungry. But

the ones about things I needed to do or even the dinner I was planning for the family grabbed me. The exercise ended and I was caught up in that thought.

T: Were you able to start the exercise up again?

C: Yes.

T: The thing I really want you to take away from this exercise is the moment when you are caught up in a thought. Notice how that thought grabbed you and pulled you in. Is that like other events in your life?

C: Certainly. It's similar to when I feel angry. When I feel angry, I also really buy into that feeling and my actions come right from anger. It's consuming.

T: Could you see a benefit to being able to watch that anger like you watched the thoughts in this exercise?

C: Totally.

T: OK. That is our goal for this week. I would like you to do two things. Please do this exercise for 10 minutes every day. This will give you practice observing when you get sucked into a thought. I'd also like you to pay attention to times during the day when you are getting pulled into a thought. Please notice it is happening and make a choice to observe that thought, rather than be pulled into it.

WRAP UP WITH HOMEWORK

You will use the same behavioral commitment worksheet you gave your client last week (refer to Behavioral Commitment Worksheet in Appendix C). Select a behavioral commitment that will allow your client to practice the skills covered in this session. It could be the exact same task as the one assigned in the previous session—focusing on the same ACT process—if your client struggled with it last week, the same task but focused on a different process of change, or a different task altogether. Link the behavioral commitments to the exercises covered in session so your client can spend more time playing around with the skills taught and figuring out how to practice them most effectively. Usually, we select the exercise that the client was most able to connect with and have the client work on the behavioral commitment while using the specific skill. For example, if your client struggles with social anxiety and wants to reach out to friends more often, the behavioral commitment can be "Ask friends to hang out via text twice this week." Within this commitment, instruct your client to practice being self-compassionate in response to thoughts and feelings that show up: "As you work on this goal, your mind is probably going to tell you 'you're not good enough' or 'no one likes you.' See if you can treat yourself kindly even when your mind feeds you these thoughts, just like you would treat a friend who believed they were not good enough or not worth being around." Be flexible when setting homework with your client and bear in mind the homework tips provided at the end of Chapter 5. For example, the client might call three people to go to a movie and all say no. The client did great and followed through on the behavioral commitment. We cannot control outcomes. The client can either stop here because the commitment was followed, or try something else consistent with the value of being around friends.

SUMMARY

Hopefully, the client is growing in psychological flexibility. In this chapter we addressed many aspects of the acceptance and mindfulness side of the six processes of change. The client should be growing in their ability to be present in the world and with themselves, see their thoughts as thoughts, and allow them to be there when useful. We also spent time linking our work to client values. Each client will shift at their own rate. Use of assessment tools such as the ACT ADVISOR (Figure 2.2) will help you track growth in these processes.

8

Sessions 7 and 8

Acceptance, Defusion, Mindfulness, and Self-as-Context

OPENING WITH A MINDFULNESS EXERCISE

Opening sessions with a mindfulness exercise is something many ACT therapists routinely do. It is not for every therapist or every client, but it is a good skill to have in your repertoire. We find this to be especially useful when the therapist or client starts the session in an emotional place. For example, it makes sense if the client enters the session and is frustrated or not being present because of something they went through, such as a difficult drive to the session or some other event they just attended. Similarly, if the therapist just had a hard session and does not feel ready to be fully present for the next session, an exercise like this can make a lot of sense. In that case, the therapist would benefit from the exercise, too. It is beneficial because it gives the therapist and client the opportunity to focus on therapy and create space from what was occurring prior to the session. If this is something you or the client find useful, you can do it at the beginning of most sessions.

As always, it is a good idea to provide some context to the exercise so the client does not misinterpret it as a way to relax or avoid. Remind the client that the point of this brief exercise is to be present with their goals in therapy and get ready for the session. It is not about making any particular feeling go away. It is about shifting focus away from the events the client was just dealing with and toward the therapy session. We generally say something like:

> I'd like to do an exercise with you to get ready for our session. I don't know if you ever feel caught up in other things when the session starts, but it certainly happens to me. I sometimes find that a little "getting present" exercise helps me to focus on the session rather than whatever topic I was dealing with prior to the session. We'll do a short exercise to help us focus on this therapy session. The goal is just to get into this room. I am not trying to help you feel relaxed or get rid of any thoughts. I am certainly not trying to

hypnotize you. I am simply trying to help us shift from whatever tasks we were working on just before this session to what we are here to work on. Do you have any thoughts or questions?

We usually keep this type of opening mindfulness exercise fairly short: between 1 and 5 minutes. Like typical mindfulness meditation exercises, we usually ask the client to be in a comfortable and alert position and to close their eyes or have their eyes rest on a spot a few feet in front of them on the floor. During the exercise, we have the client shift their attention to notice a variety of experiences in the present moment in a defused, accepting way. We use a slow, calm tone and pace to elicit a mindful presence in the room. We also use prompts to guide clients to bring mindful qualities to whatever they are noticing (e.g., being curious, descriptive, accepting, defused).

Listed next are common experiences we would prompt a client to notice in the exercise, typically including three to six of these things depending on time and how much you want to emphasize broad flexibility versus targeted focus.

- Notice the breath: You might prompt them to notice aspects such as the sensations of their stomach or chest rising and falling, sensations of air coming in through their nose and down their throat, the change in temperature in the air as it enters and leaves their body, the point where they finish breathing in and begin breathing out.
- Notice sensations in specific parts of the body: You might prompt them to notice the feelings of their feet contacting the floor, their body contacting the chair, their hands, their head, and so on, and to look for specific types of sensations such as tension and temperature.
- Notice sounds in the room: Notice specific sounds, like the sound machine or air vents, or look for more subtle sounds.
- Notice thoughts: Notice thoughts in a defused way by simply labeling them as thoughts or watching them pass by like clouds in the sky or leaves floating down a stream (you can be creative with the analogy you use here).
- Notice any feelings or urges: Notice any feelings or urges right now in an accepting way that simply treats them for what they are. You might ask the client to notice where it shows up in their body and the sensations associated with it.
- Take perspective on the past: You might have them practice shifting perspectives, looking out from their own eyes as they went about their morning routine or traveled to the session.
- Take perspective on the future: You might have them picture what they will see when they open their eyes and return to the session or what they will be doing later in the session or after it.
- Notice the observing perspective (self-as-context): Notice there is a "you" noticing all of these experiences that is separate from and

watching these experiences come and go, a "you behind your eyes noticing everything."

- Notice your intentions (values): Consider what you want to be about over the next 45 minutes of therapy and how you want to engage in the session. What could this time be about for you?

REVIEW HOMEWORK

As always, check in on homework from the previous session. You might have a relatively formulaic way of going about this. Be sure to cover the core points of the homework review: (1) your client's direct experience of engaging in meaningful action and (2) the internal experiences that showed up as they worked on this behavioral commitment. This check-in—even if brief—is important for helping you start to assess where your client is at in terms of the six processes of change and potentially for determining the areas on which you will focus more this session.

We hope the client will have engaged in the mindfulness exercise for 10 minutes per day. Ask the client how often they actually practiced, what they found useful about the exercise, and what part or parts they found difficult. It is also useful to know if practicing the exercise led to any changes in their day-to-day experience. Maybe they were able to notice an inner experience building up and could do so before reactively responding to it. If the client did find it useful, you may suggest that they continue to practice mindfulness exercises. There are a handful of mindfulness apps clients might find useful. These apps typically provide guided meditations and mindfulness exercises. A list of mindfulness apps is provided in Appendix D at the end of this book.

ASSESS WHERE THE CLIENT STRUGGLED AND TOUCH ON ACCEPTANCE AND DEFUSION

Just like in previous sessions, use the client's experience to help you figure out areas where the client could use some assistance. We recommend using the ACT ADVISOR (Figure 2.2) to organize your assessment and ensure that you consider all six ACT processes. Ask the client about a situation in which they struggled over the last week. We are not looking for a situation that was externally difficult, like a large work task, but something more emotionally difficult (although sometimes these can overlap). You can say, "Tell me about an instance where your thoughts, feelings, or sensations were a problem for you." Then, once the client provides an instance that they struggled with, dig deeply into that instance. Help the client come in contact with the ways in which they are responding to their inner experiences in those situations. Once you feel that the client is properly in contact with what it felt like in that situation, move into an appropriate defusion or acceptance exercise. You might have already realized this: Knowing what the "appropriate" exercise is requires you to track how your client responds to previous exercises. Even then, therapists are not all-knowing and may not always perfectly predict what will work for their clients. Remember that you get to model psychological flexibility too by trying out new exercises and being willing to shift examples when current ones are not working out. The following is a brief exchange that will remind you of what we are getting at.

THERAPIST (T): Please tell me about a situation in the last week where your thoughts, feelings, or bodily sensations got in the way.

CLIENT (C): I have a good one. I was fixing a screen at my house. As I say that out loud, I feel stupid that it became such a mess. Anyway, I was trying to get a new screen into the frame, and of course it is not going well at all. My husband is off doing something fun in the house. If you've ever put in a new screen, you know how poorly that all works. It's so complicated. As I struggle to get the new screen in, my feelings of frustration just keep increasing. Then I start to have negative thoughts about the whole house and how little help my husband is giving me. I do believe he could help more, but that was not really the issue at the time. It was just that the screen was making me mad, and I was also getting mad at his not helping me out—even though I know now it wasn't about that. Eventually, he comes by and asks how the screen is going. Instead of saying, "It is difficult," I snap and say something like, "Nothing gets done around here unless I ask," and "I'm tired of being the only one who takes care of these tasks," and so on.

T: How did things go between you two?

C: It was not good, but it was also not the worst. He got frustrated and I said some other things I wish I would not have said. But we worked through it in the end.

T: Values-wise, is that how you would have liked to deal with that situation?

C: Not at all. I am fine with chatting with him about how we help each other, but that whole thing had to do with my anger around the stupid task I was doing. I really didn't have an issue with how much he helps around the house. I mean, I do wish he would help more, but at that moment, it was not an issue and not something I would have brought up.

T: Tell me about how you responded to the frustration you were experiencing while trying to fix that screen.

C: It overwhelmed me. It was not "just a thought I was having"; it engulfed me.

T: Were you OK with those feelings being there?

C: No, I experienced them pretty negatively and wanted them to go away. Even in the way that I yelled at my husband, it was just a way to deal with the frustration I was feeling.

T: Do you wish you had handled your frustration differently?

C: Of course I do.

T: OK, let's do a little exercise with the thoughts and feelings you are having right now. Instead of evaluating them as good or bad or trying to keep or push them away, let's look at them like this . . .

Annoying younger sibling defusion/acceptance exercise

The goal of this exercise is to create some distance from thoughts by treating them like an annoying younger sibling and to foster acceptance by seeing thoughts as children who do not really think through their actions. If your client does not have a younger sibling, you can use a younger cousin, a neighbor's child, a friend's child, or any other child in their life as an example. The following text introduces this exercise.

T: I remember growing up with my younger brother and being annoyed with him all the time. He would always pester me and try to get my attention. But one day, I had this great idea to respond minimally to what he had to say. He would come up to me and keep asking me, "Hey, what are you doing?" over and over again. And I would just acknowledge him and continue watching TV. Now, I think of that response as just what I want clients to do with their thoughts. Maybe our thoughts are like younger siblings and many of the things our younger siblings say are unimportant. What are some of your thoughts that just pop up out of nowhere and sort of catch you off guard?

C: Most of mine are around my body. You know, "you're fat," "people are looking at your fat," "these clothes don't fit," and so on.

T: If you really thought about these thoughts, are they more like little brother comments or more like your parents' trying to be helpful?

C: They are more like a little kid. They just come out of nowhere and I'd be better off treating them like you did.

T: Excellent. Can you describe what this kid looks like?

C: Oh, easy. It's a little bossy girl who thinks she knows it all. [The therapist can keep prompting and gaining information on this kid.]

T: I'd like you to practice treating thoughts about your looks like a younger sibling yelling at you. I don't see this as a life answer to your issues, but maybe interacting with your thoughts in this way will make it a little easier to ignore that thought in the same way I ignored my younger brother when we were growing up.

NOTE acronym

At this point, it helps to summarize all the skills clients have been learning to apply to new situations and challenges that arise. We typically find that a combination of ACT skills are relevant to many situations clients encounter, including attending to the present, defusing from unhelpful thoughts, accepting difficult internal experiences without engaging in experiential avoidance, and identifying and engaging in valued actions. We provide an acronym here that can help clients practice noticing an unhelpful cycle, using acceptance and defusion skills, identifying relevant values, and doing what matters. The following is a way of introducing this acronym to your client.

> Here is a way to summarize the skills we've been talking about in therapy. When you find yourself getting caught up in unhelpful patterns with your thoughts and feelings, you can return to your NOTE. NOTE stands for **n**oticing what is happening, **o**bserving your thoughts and feelings for what they are, **t**urning toward your values, and **e**ngaging in what matters. You can think of NOTE as like a reminder note you set for yourself, but in this case the reminder is to practice what we have been doing in therapy. The first step when you are getting stuck is to notice it. You need to first catch the pattern occurring to make a change. Once you do, you can practice observing your thoughts and feelings for what they are without fighting with them or buying into them. This can help break the unhelpful pattern and give some space to turn toward your values, considering what is important to you and how you want to act in the moment. Finally, engage in what matters by doing something that fits with your values. Sometimes that might be walking away for a moment to stop an unhelpful cycle, but the idea is you are making an intentional choice to move toward your values and what is effective, rather than continuing in a cycle where your thoughts and feelings are the ones dictating what you do. Let's try this now with the experience you talked about having with your husband. What might it have looked like to practice NOTE?

We have provided a handout for NOTE you can share with your clients in Appendix E.

INTRODUCE SELF-AS-CONTEXT

Self-as-context (or observer self) is probably the ACT process of change that confuses the most people. But it really is not that complicated. In short, it is defusion applied to self-evaluations or self-stories. One might wonder why we don't just have five processes of change and talk about other ways to do defusion. While that is reasonable, there are enough instances where self-evaluations or self-conceptualizations really get in the way for the client. We often see this with clients diagnosed with generalized anxiety disorder (GAD). The client might say, "I am a worrier. I am the one who takes care of things for the family and without me they would all be lost." Thus, when this client has the thought, "I always take care of my family," it feels powerful and particularly meaningful. In many ways, the thought defines who they are. Self-as-context provides a different perspective, as simply an observer of all of one's inner experiences, including one's self-stories, rather than overly identifying with them. By doing so, clients may be able to simply notice their self-stories as distinct from the "self" and act in ways that deviate from their self-conceptualizations when doing so serves their values. For example, the person diagnosed with GAD may choose to take a day off from household chores and go for a hike, even when doing so appears to contradict the story that they "always take care of their family."

We have also done a fair amount of work with the U.S. Army, and treating "wounded warriors" is a huge part of serving those who were in combat. Many, but not all, individuals who are in the Army see themselves as "strong, protectors, and soldiers." If a person experiences a grave enough injury, they may not be able to serve as a soldier anymore. That identifying label can be lost. Their injury might also be notable enough that they do not feel strong or like a protector anymore. Self-labels are interesting. For some, their labels keep them moving forward, and for others, the labels stop them from moving. If the labels move clients in the directions they value, there is less to address clinically. But for those whose labels stop them from moving in their valued directions, creating some defusion around those labels (or creating a self as the context where inner experiences occur) can benefit them. Presenting this concept can be useful for all clients, especially those who struggle with self-conceptualizations.

It helps to spend time on self-as-context if you hear your client talk about self-evaluations in a way that holds them back. There are two main ways this happens. The first is the more obvious: the self-evaluation is "negative" and therefore stops the person. For example, "I'm too shy to do that," "I have an anxiety disorder so this is just how it is," or "This is just the way people in my family are." If you hear a client state something about themselves that seems to stop them from moving toward their values, it is worth spending time on self-as-context.

Similarly, a client will sometimes have a self-evaluation that is generally supportive and helpful. However, rigidly following or protecting that self-evaluation in all circumstances can lead to actions that are inconsistent with values. One example that occurs for me (M.P.T.) is I see myself as wise about my area of research. I have a sense of competency and mastery in this area. I find the confidence actually makes giving talks easier. Thus, this self-evaluation is helpful for me 90% of the time. The time when I find it is not helpful is when I feel challenged on my knowledge of my research areas. I will feel a pull to defend my position. Even though I do not act on this pull, my self-evaluation is still getting challenged and I feel a need to protect it. So, when a self-evaluation is helpful, it is functional to listen to it or even feel motivated by it. But when that same self-evaluation is not helpful, it is useful to simply recognize that it is occurring and choose not to listen to it. Thus, if I am giving a talk and an audience member offers an alternative way of looking at things, I may benefit from noticing that my self-evaluation is being challenged, allowing that feeling to be there, and listening to the audience member. Thus, self-evaluations are neither good nor bad; they can be helpful or unhelpful and that depends on the time and situation. It is up to the therapist to help the client recognize when to listen to them and when to politely ignore them.

We suggest starting by discussing how the client's self-evaluations help or hold them back. After the client seems to understand the topic and sees why you are bringing it up, move on to an exercise that gets at self-as-context. Here is what the discussion might look like:

T: I want to talk about how we see ourselves. Our self-evaluations can push us in different directions. Sometimes these evaluations push us in the directions we are interested in going and sometimes that is not the case. Do you have any big self-evaluations?

C: That is a good question. The one most pertinent to what we are working on is my thoughts about how "I'm damaged." It's something I have felt ever since my childhood. You know, things were pretty messed up then. Then, as I got older I had struggles in life. I've always felt it was because of my messed-up childhood. So, that's me. I feel like I'm damaged and that feeling certainly has affected me throughout life.

T: Thanks for telling me that. That is the type of thing I was talking about. Tell me about a time when that thought affected you in a way you did not like.

C: Sure. Recently, when I was dating this guy, things were not going perfectly. We had our struggles, but overall things were pretty good. But whenever things were not perfect, I would blame myself for being "damaged." I'd have thoughts like, "Well, this is how things are going to go for you because you don't understand healthy relationships."

T: How do those thoughts affect you?

C: At times, I notice they are automatic. They don't really mean anything and are just sort of thoughts that happen for me. But there are also other times when I totally buy into them and I can almost convince myself I don't deserve a good relationship or allow myself to act in ways that I don't want, just because I don't believe I deserve to have a good relationship. I guess those thoughts sometimes get in my way.

T: Hmm, this seems pretty important. Do you feel this self-evaluation about "being damaged" is a big deal in your life or a small issue?

C: I'd say it is a pretty big thing.

T: Like if it was a dog, would it be a Rottweiler or a miniature poodle?

C: It's the big dog.

T: OK, so maybe we need to figure out what to do with this one.

C: Yes.

T: Maybe think about it like this . . .

You are not your thoughts, like a house is not its furniture

The purpose of this exercise is to help the client see their thoughts or other inner experiences as events that occur within them rather than define them. This concept can be presented in the following way.

T: Sometimes people really get pushed around by their thoughts, especially thoughts about themselves. But maybe these thoughts we have about ourselves are less meaningful and powerful than they say they are. To start, let's be clear on a self-evaluation you have of yourself that is big and really influences you.

C: OK. I'm kind.

T: Tell me emotions you often have.

C. I am peaceful. But I'm also sad.

T: OK. Tell me some bodily sensations you often experience.

C: I have a lack of energy. I know others often have lots of energy, but I always feel drained.

T: This is all very interesting. We could keep going with things you experience. We could talk about feelings you have, thoughts you have, how your body works, and so on. But not one of these things is you. It's sort of like a house. What is a house? [Give the client time to talk about houses. Interestingly, there are many types of houses.] What is usually in a house? [Similarly, there are many things in houses. Some houses are very empty and some are very full.] What happens in a house? [Some houses are busy, have businesses, and some are empty most of the year.] Here is my point: A house is no more the building, the items in it, or the actions that take place in it than you are your thoughts, feelings, and actions. What if you see yourself as the place where all these events occur but not as the events themselves? Just like your house is still your house, even if you repainted the walls and switched out the furniture. Would you still be you if you had different thoughts, feeling, emotions, or bodily sensations?

C: Of course.

T: So, if these things don't define you, do you have more choice in how you act? Just like, could I decorate my house like a cabin or an '80s night club?

C: Yes.

T: This week I'd like you to think of your thoughts, feelings, and bodily sensations as events that occur within you—like items in your house. Let's see if that changes how those inner experiences affect you.

WRAP UP WITH HOMEWORK

This week, you would likely want your client to practice self-as-context or taking the stance of an observer of their inner experiences rather than identifying with them. You can still build on behavioral commitments from previous weeks and add on a self-as-context exercise for your client to work on over the next week. For example, if your client has been working on practicing defusion from worries by acting inconsistently with the worries and finds it helpful to continue doing that, use that as one of the behavioral commitments. Once you have determined the parameters for the first behavioral commitment, you can set up the second task.

T: Great, so we will continue practicing defusion with breaking your worry rules. I'd also like you to practice some of what we talked about today in terms of seeing yourself as the house for your thoughts and feelings. How would you like to go about that?

C: I'm not sure. Should I just sit down for 5 minutes and do a mindfulness meditation?

T: We could definitely do that. We could also focus on using this skill with a specific behavioral commitment like what we've been doing for other sessions. For example, we've talked about your story that you have to take care of everyone and how this story means you have to pick up after everyone else and make sure everyone gets to where they need to be.

C: Oh, yeah. That story keeps me so busy. It's exhausting.

T: What would it be like to see that story as another piece of furniture in your house? Maybe it is the grand piano passed down in your family for generations. It feels big and important. It feels like you need to listen to it. At the same time, you get to be so much more than an old piano, simply by noticing you are the house containing it.

C: Yeah, that might be a helpful way to see things. Let's do that instead.

With two behavioral commitments, feel free to use two copies of the *Behavioral Commitment Worksheet* (see Appendix C) so that the parameters of the assignment are clear to both you and your client. Make sure the process to be practiced with each task is explicitly stated.

SESSION SUMMARY

In this session you will have further practiced acceptance and defusion with your client and introduced self-as-context work to target unhelpful self-stories. You should have continued identifying areas of growth while reviewing the homework and using the ACT ADVISOR to guide your assessment. You should have also tailored your focus on acceptance, defusion, and self-as-context in this session, based on relevance to your client. Finally, you need to have assigned them homework related to practicing self-as-context. The goal for this session is to build on skills previously learned while adding to their psychological flexibility repertoire by introducing self-as-context.

9

Session 9

Values

REVIEW HOMEWORK

At the beginning of the session, ask your client how their homework went. Last session, you introduced the idea of the observer self or self-as-context, so be sure to check in on how your client put their understanding of this ACT process into practice. Did they notice their thoughts as things that come and go in their mind? Did they loosen their grip on unhelpful self-identities? Did they act independently of labels that would otherwise have kept them stagnant? If your client was unable to take the perspective of an observer self this past week, return to the previous chapter and go over self-as-context with them again. If you notice the issue has more to do with acceptance or being present, return to the relevant chapter.

As with every homework review, this is your chance to assess where your client is on each process of change. You should be able to complete the ACT ADVISOR (Figure 2.2) for the client sitting in front of you. If you have doubts about where your client lands on any of the processes, ask them questions. You need to know where your client is at on each of the processes to determine what you do in your session. We recommend strengthening your client's skills in other areas (acceptance and mindfulness processes) before moving on to values clarification. As we discuss later, this is because a client who is experientially avoidant, cognitively fused, stuck in the past, or overly attached to self-labels may struggle with honestly identifying areas of life that are personally meaningful to them.

CLARIFYING VALUES

Values work, or talking about values, can increase engagement in therapy, but the ultimate goal of clarifying values is to increase clients' awareness of what truly matters to them so they have a meaningful direction in which to move. This work comes from research showing that the function or effect of target events will change depending on the events with which they are verbally associated. For example, if the client is engaging in a pattern of action that is not working to achieve their goals, it is likely because verbal rules tell the client this pattern leads to something important to them. Even though abusing substances ultimately takes a person away from their long-term values, it probably takes the person toward something meaningful in the short term. Maybe it is peace of mind, a break from life, a supportive social group—there is something reinforcing about that action. There is no link between the immediate actions in which the person engages and the long-term values the person cares about. Values link immediate actions to larger things that are meaningful to people. For example, you might do a simple work task to get someone off your back or to check it off your to-do list. But linking that small task to something meaningful—such as earning money for the family, doing a coworker a favor, being part of a team—can make it more motivating.

One reason it is so difficult to engage in tasks where the outcome is delayed—or never occurs—is the reward is not immediately present. It is easier to do things that give us a reward quickly (like ordering a burger at a fast-food restaurant) than to wait for a reward for our actions (like ordering a burger and hearing it will take a week to get to us). However, we do not always get the feedback we are used to or like. For example, if I am kind to my wife, she appreciates it and will often tell me, whereas my children do not know how to do that yet. I might help them with homework or a school project and not even get a "thank you"; instead, I get anger and maybe a little crying. The reward for helping my children with homework is way off in the future. It might be when they get into college, graduate from college, or do something else that requires knowledge. Thus, it is easy to make doing homework about getting it out of the way for the night so they make it through school the next day. If doing homework with my children could be tied to helping them have a meaningful career or a happy life, then it becomes more meaningful in the moment.

To get this concept, think about something you do that you find immediately unpleasant but you know is the choice you want to make in the long term. It could be saying no to dessert, waking up early to go to the gym, or hiking in the dark to catch a sunrise. You will not see the benefit immediately but you believe it will be there in the future, and that makes doing the task worth it to you. These are examples of goals or values, and they provide motivation for present actions.

The other core aspect of values discussions is to help the client decide among the many choices they have. In any situation, we have the opportunity to engage in various actions and, unfortunately, we often choose the one that is most immediately rewarding, even when it does not serve our values. Values clarity helps increase the importance of one set of actions over another. Specifically, we aim to make immediate actions that support values more rewarding while making actions tied to being psychologically inflexible less rewarding. As a simple example, take a college student who has homework to complete but is also offered the opportunity to watch videos on their computer. They can choose to engage in an immediately reinforcing action and emotionally disengage, or emotionally engage (which takes effort) and work on their studies. One action is immediately rewarding, whereas the other is less so; one has long-term value and the other may not. If the student can connect with what is meaningful to them about their studies, maybe doing homework will become more rewarding. For example, if the student could think about the career their degree will offer, the family they could support with a stable career, and the freedom the career will give them, then working on homework might be more meaningful relative to watching videos, especially if watching videos then becomes associated with moving away from a fulfilling future.

The concept of values can be new and confusing to clients, so we like to walk them through it in a straightforward way. Here are steps we usually follow when working on values with a client. In a previously published chapter we wrote, we offered the following steps for starting to address values: (1) creating defusion from social rules, (2) defining values as a concept, (3) defining personal values, (4) choosing values, (5) determining the consistency of current actions with values, (6) choosing goals consistent with values, and (7) behaving in accordance with goals and values (Twohig & Crosby, 2008). In the following outline, we will walk through how you could introduce values to a client.

1. CREATING DEFUSION FROM SOCIAL RULES

Part of the conceptualization of values is that they need to be intrinsically motivating to the client. Things we "should" do offer a moderate level of motivation, whereas things we sincerely care about offer a high level of motivation. Thus, we would like the client's actions to be tied to things they genuinely care about in order to achieve maximum motivation for action. We need to clarify values because many clients have not thought deeply about what they value or say they value things that others want or that seem like "correct" values. It may be helpful to watch out for externally determined values as they will not imbue clients' lives with meaning and purpose and do not have the same motivating quality as freely chosen values. Depending on the client, disentangling imposed from true values may take time.

Clients generally will have followed patterns that work for them and connected with values occasionally but do a mediocre job of linking actions to values. To help the client consistently link actions to values, we need to help them become aware of the elements of life that create their values, and offer some level of choice as to which values they want to pursue. Remember, defusion is about seeing inner experiences as they are, rather than as real things. Thus, a person may choose to follow a thought or not when they are practicing defusion. Thoughts are still relevant when someone is defused; defusion simply allows us to see our thoughts more objectively. Defusion cannot detach us from the social or cultural context that helped shape our values, but it does allow us to decide which values we ultimately choose to follow. Intentionally identifying and pursuing values means we might choose to keep certain patterns we have adopted in life and stop other patterns we do not want to keep upon consideration. We are deliberately not giving examples in this text, to highlight that values are chosen by the client, not the therapist, though there are moments when a therapist should step in and clarify the client's value; this will be covered later in the chapter.

In the following text, we go over how one might start this conversation with a client.

I would like to have a conversation about how we came to care about certain things, enjoy a set of activities, participate in the groups we are in, or have the political or religious leanings we have. What things in life have influenced you most? [Have a discussion about this. There is no right answer. We want the client to think about what influences them.]

Tell me how these parts of your life have influenced you in ways you are proud of? Also, tell me how these things have affected you in ways you are not proud of? [Again, there is no right or wrong answer. We just want the client to see that their values are influenced by broader things in life.]

If you were to do something different in life, who would be proud of you, and who would be upset with you for making that change? [We are trying to help the client see that these external variables can be helpful in following values but can also hold them back.]

And how would you feel about others' reactions to this change?

Here is why I am asking you all these questions. Today, we are going to talk about things that are important to you deep down. I hope we can spend time today discussing these things and how much time you are spending on them. Obviously, our interests and values have to come from somewhere. This is a wonderful thing because it allows us to share interests and heritage with family and friends. But part of this can be difficult for some people. Sometimes, we hope for things that go against our rules about the way things are supposed to be. Sometimes, what we want in the moment is inconsistent with our true values. And there are times when we are interested in something but it goes against the shared interests of our social group or family. [Again, we are not giving examples so as not to limit the scope of this discussion to our own cultural context.] What are some areas of your life where there are strong expectations and your views don't match up with those perfectly?

2. DEFINING VALUES AS A CONCEPT

We like to think of targeting values as an action in which the therapist engages. Targeting values involves anything that increases engagement in therapy and behavior change. We usually think of this as linking current actions to delayed but important outcomes. However, it can also include linking current actions to smaller positive outcomes that might occur relatively soon but are delayed from the moment the value-consistent action occurs. As therapists, we like to hear about someone valuing their family and choosing to do things for them. But we have also had the adolescent client who is not that in tune with these larger values and currently cares about dating, friends, or popularity. We are fine with linking important therapy actions to these more immediate and smaller values as long as they facilitate engagement in therapy. For example, I had a young client with trichotillomania who initially said she really cared about being pretty. While that may not sound like an intrinsically meaningful reason for engaging in therapy, it mattered to this client and motivated her. Therefore, we used that as a motivator for our initial sessions. As we got further into therapy, we started to focus on larger values that were longer-lasting, such as education and relationships. The reason we are highlighting this issue is that values are functionally defined. That means what the values are is less important than what the values do for the client. Values work in ACT involves discussions about topics that increase engagement in therapy and related actions. There are a couple other points to consider, but you can glean them from this description we would use with a client:

> We have been working on many things throughout therapy, such as how to deal with your thoughts and feelings, and how to change your actions even when your feelings are not on board. While we may not have chatted about this a lot, we have been working on these other things in the hope that they will allow you to make meaningful changes in your life. We are not about noticing our thoughts as thoughts for its own sake. I mean, maybe it is nice, but we want larger changes. I like to think of the reason we work in therapy is so that we can pursue our values. Values are things we care about; they are things that are important to us. They may not line up with how we live or what we do, but they are what we care about. For example, I might value taking care of the planet but not work at it every day. Conversely, I also value family and get the chance to show that value each day. We might even value things without doing anything about them ever or for a very long time. Just because you are inactive in that area does not change how important it is to you.
>
> Values are different from goals. A goal is an action you can accomplish, such as graduating from college. In contrast, a value is larger and can always be pursued—even though how you pursue it will change over time. For example, I value education, but as a professor I pursue that value differently from when I was a student. Similarly, I might be a great dad and help with the science fair project and spend one-on-one time with my kids. Then, the next day rolls around and I have the opportunity to practice being a great dad again. Things will change over our lives, and our values could shift or the way we pursue our values could change. My children need different things from me each year, and maybe one day they will have families of their own and I will parent my children differently.
>
> The last important thing is something we just discussed: There are no right or wrong values. These are things you care about and want to spend your

time on. I bet they will be different from the things I value, and I do not judge you for that. People sometimes worry that they have a "bad" value. That is not something that comes up. All our values come from somewhere. They might be from your family, friends, religion, television, whatever. Sometimes we choose the same values as those of the people around us, and sometimes we don't. Depending on the situation, this can be easy or difficult. Sometimes our values are part of a larger group or culture, and there are costs to having the same ones or to not having the same ones. Remember, valuing something is the first step; choosing how you are going to show it is another one. You might value something but choose not to act on it because of practical life issues. That happens, and we can talk about it. For right now, tell me about the things that are most important to you.

3. DEFINING PERSONAL VALUES

Now that we have helped the client understand what values are, it is worthwhile to help the client think about what they value. As mentioned earlier, clients may be able to readily list values, but it is worth exploring if these are truly meaningful directions or if they are more rules for clients to follow. One way to elucidate this distinction is to ask, "If no one else knew you were doing these actions, would you still do them?" Behaviors that are about values will still be important to the client even without external reward, because values are by definition intrinsically motivating. Take your time in working with your client to identify their values; the foundation for values clarification is the acceptance and mindfulness processes, so the discussion may be muddled or fused if clients have not practiced those processes sufficiently. For example, clients may insist they value a certain domain, even when they dread situations associated with it and cannot articulate why it matters to them. In these instances, returning to defusion from social rules or willingness to be with discomfort (e.g., guilt, shame) may, in turn, bring greater clarity to what their values really are.

There are many forms already created that are useful in helping clients understand that there are many areas one can value. There are a couple versions for this that many people use, but this list is far from exhaustive. We like the Valued Living Questionnaire (VLQ; Wilson, Sandoz, Kitchens, & Roberts, 2010) and the Bull's-Eye Values Survey (BEVS; Lundgren, Luoma, Dahl, Strosahl, & Melin, 2012). Both are validated measures with scoring systems, but they also work well as clinical devices to help clients understand values work.

Valued Living Questionnaire (VLQ)

We like the VLQ because it facilitates a longer discussion of the client's valued areas of life. The VLQ lists 10 life domains most people tend to value. The client is asked to talk about how they would define their value in each of the areas. This is interesting, because most people don't have strong values in all 10 areas. As the client talks through each of the areas, it helps to reiterate that we do not have to value everything. In this particular phase, we are only defining what each area means to us. Help the client define them in big-picture terms rather than as a set of behaviors or goals. Let's take "Friendships/Social relations" for example; rather than saying "spend time with friends every week" we are looking for something larger, like "Being there for my friends during good and bad times." It is fine if a client says a specific area is not important to them. It is your job as the therapist to help the client clarify what they value in each domain. This discussion can take awhile.

Bull's-Eye Values Survey (BEVS)

Although the BEVS has fewer items than the VLQ, it is broader in scope. You would have the same conversation as you would with the VLQ. Ask the client to discuss what they care about in each of the four areas. Remind them you are looking for overarching descriptions rather than specific actions.

Many of you will work in clinics that see individuals with similar backgrounds. There might be a set of values more relevant to your clients, and you can adjust these main areas accordingly. You may even cross out the existing ones and write in different ones if that makes more sense for your client.

4. CHOOSING HOW MUCH SOMETHING IS VALUED

After valued areas have been defined, work with the client on gauging how much they value each area. For many values, this will be easy for the client. They will know where they stand on many of these areas and feel comfortable about it. On occasion, there will be an internal conflict with respect to how much they care about a specific area. The client may have been engaging in activities in that area but finding that those activities do not really fit the value. Maybe there was pressure from an outside person or group that they should value something, but the client does not feel that way deep down. This can be quite complicated. Sometimes the conflict between outside pressures and personal beliefs comes from something the client really cares about, such as culture, family, or religion. A perfect answer to this situation does not exist. But this is why we do a fuller examination of values closer to the end of therapy. If the acceptance and mindfulness processes (acceptance, defusion, self-as-context, and being present) have been covered, an open discussion about this conflict can occur. We are referring to significant conflicts, such as current culture conflicting with goals taken from a previous culture, or personal views that differ from religious views—the big stuff. This internal struggle of actually being able to pursue all our values at once shows up for everyone. When the client brings up that issue, make sure to validate it. However, stay focused on how much they care about each thing for now.

In the next section, we will talk about how much time we are going to choose to spend on each valued domain. This conversation can be carried out with the aid of the VLQ or BEVS or through an open discussion. We offer here a description of how this might sound:

> We just spent some time discussing what each of these areas means to you. I think you did a nice job figuring that out. It can be a little difficult because many people have not thought about what they truly care about in awhile. Also, what we care about changes with time. We have new priorities or maybe start to value different things. Again, I think you did a nice job wading through some of that. Next, I'd like to talk about how much you care about—or value—each of these areas. I'd like you to tell me whether you value this at a low or high level. We can also go from 1 to 10, whatever you like. I just want you to have the opportunity to tell me how important each of these areas is to you.
>
> There is one catch here. I want honest answers from you. This can be difficult because there are lots of pressures inside your head as we talk about this. As we talked about earlier, there were many people and groups telling you how things should be. This is a wonderful and problematic thing—like the chatter in our minds. Some of the suggestions you have received in life fit for you and some don't. Maybe some don't fit for you but they are still honestly important to you. I can't be in your head, but I want you to try and be honest with yourself as you rate these areas. I fully expect it to be a little difficult and for there to be a little struggle in your head as you rate some of these areas. We are not talking about changing any actions at this time, so there is no consequence to what you say. It might be useful to think of answering these questions as if nobody was listening and nobody would judge.

Our only warning is to not judge the client's choices. This is a discussion. The client has been working through these issues in their head for a while, and it would be a shame if the first time they admitted it aloud they were shot down. Validate the emotional struggle that is occurring; you do not have to validate the action. There will be a little more on this at the end of this chapter in the section on "problematic" values.

5. DETERMINING THE CONSISTENCY OF CURRENT ACTIONS WITH VALUES

The next step is easily covered using the VLQ or BEVS. The VLQ has one sheet where the client rates how much they care about each of the values. There is a second sheet, which looks the same as the first except the instructions ask how well their actions match how much they care about their value. It is basically asking, "Based on how much you care about this issue, how well are you doing on a daily basis?" This is where all the previous discussions start to pay off. Hopefully, the client understands that values are complicated and that they change throughout life. They are based on our histories and individual differences, and we can use them to guide us when making large and small decisions. Again, if some of the acceptance and mindfulness processes are in place, then the client is more likely to be honest about where their actions and their values do not line up. We would describe this to the client as follows:

> You could probably guess this next step was coming, but now let's look at how your values and day-to-day actions line up. We just talked about how much you value each of the areas we defined. Now let's talk about how well your actions match up with how much you care about the various areas. This can be a little tricky, but you will get it. Let's say you value something very little and you spend no time on that value. In that case, your values and your actions line up. Now, if you value something highly, and you spend next to no time in that area, your values and actions don't line up. There can also be a midway situation, where you might value something a lot, and do a little in that area, but not quite as much as you'd like. Then this is an area for some improvement.
>
> Going over this can be difficult for some people. It can have its re-warding moments—like when you notice that you are doing really well in an area. But there will also be times when you feel uncomfortable be-cause your actions and your values don't match. I have a couple thoughts about that. First, be easy on yourself. We all do this. Nobody's values and actions line up perfectly. Second, maybe living in that state of tension be-tween how you choose to live and your values is the best place to be. If you were to go 100% into any value, there would not be enough time or energy to do the other ones as fully as you want. Maybe that is how life is. We figure out what is most important to us and do our best to meet our expectations, but we will never fully be there. Finally, that discomfort you feel from being away from where you want to be values-wise might mean something. Remember, internal experiences are indicators that something is going on. Maybe that something is meaningless, maybe you need to do the opposite of the feeling, or maybe it tells you to go for it and you can follow that emotion. The other day, I had two commitments, and had some guilt about skipping one but not about the other. When I paused to connect with my values, I could tell one was more consistent with my values and the other was more for immediate gratification, so I made a shift. In that case, the guilt signaled to me that I cared more about one of the commitments.

Let's go over each one of these values and you can rate how consistent your actions are with how important they are to you.

6. CHOOSING GOALS CONSISTENT WITH VALUES

Now that you and the client have found discrepancies between actions and values, the two of you can work on doing something about it. Ask the client to tell you about the areas where their actions and values differ. Ask them if any of these differences are meaningful to them. It is possible that the gap between their value and action is planned. Maybe things are occurring in life that makes that so. Still, a conversation about the discrepancy is meaningful.

Identify areas where the values–actions discrepancy is meaningful to the client (i.e., they want it to be different). Discuss what internal experiences are getting in the way of their pursuing the value. Also, discuss real-life issues that are in the way, such as access to things or time. The internal-experience part is important because this is where some of the psychological flexibility discussion will come in. The client should be able to describe when fear or frustration gets in the way of their being able to do the things they care about. This may lead to prolonged conversations about the acceptance and mindfulness processes.

There will also be practical challenges. To some extent, you may be able to offer some guidance on how to fix these external issues, but chances are the client has thought of many of them. Putting the ideas into action has probably been the difficult part. Most likely, inner experiences about the outside world are the largest barrier—for example, thoughts about not having enough time, not doing it well enough, or it not being time to start working on it. These are cognitions about the world that may or may not represent the way the world actually is. For example, when someone feels they do not have time, they may not have a lot of free time, but there is always time to make small changes. This is the time to help the client decide what changes to start making. It could be discussed as follows:

After looking at the differences between your values and actions, which areas do you want to work on?

What external obstacles come to mind when you think about making these changes?

What fears or other concerns come to your mind when you think about making these changes?

Let's think about small changes you can make that would move you closer to this value. It will not get you to where you want to be—which may not be possible anyway—but it will move you one step in that direction. I like to think of this as data plotted on a graph. The trend can be increasing, decreasing, or constant. We are hoping for an increase in values-consistent actions, no matter how slight. If you work at it, even slight changes will eventually add up to a lot.

7. BEHAVING IN ACCORDANCE WITH GOALS AND VALUES

In this last step, have the client agree to engage in an action that supports one of their values. When choosing this action, pick something with a 90% chance of occurring. We would greatly prefer it gets accomplished than it be huge. Also, remind the client that half the point of the behavioral commitment is to engage in more valued action, but the other half is to practice psychological flexibility skills in difficult situations. We like to remind people that they may focus on either aspect during the exercise. Sometimes, the action feels motivating. Other times, it is more aversive and it is hard for clients to connect to their value during the activity. In the latter situation, we can find meaning in building our psychological flexibility. The last thing we stress is to be flexible with the agreement. We want the client to follow through on what was agreed on, but if they cannot make the commitment happen, they can do something functionally similar. For example, if the client agrees to look into jobs but their internet is down, they could update their résumé instead.

VALUES ARE GUIDES

Our favorite aspect of values is that they can keep guiding action well past the therapy phase. Values can be used as a guide to make daily decisions. In any situation the client is in, they can ask themselves whether this action is about moving toward something meaningful (i.e., a value) or about altering some emotion. Then, they can use this information to adjust their behavior accordingly. Values are also useful when a client is stuck. During that stuck moment, the client can look at which action will further a value. All other issues aside, the client should choose the action consistent with their value.

WHAT ABOUT PROBLEMATIC VALUES?

When we are teaching at the university or are training offsite, we usually get asked what to do if a client has a value that is antisocial, such as harming children. Honestly, this is very unlikely to happen. We have never had a client who presented with such a disturbing value. If it were to happen and the disturbing value is not the result of psychological inflexibility, you are welcome to inform the client there are ethical issues in addressing that value, but they can work on many other values.

The more likely situation is the client's value comes from a psychologically in-flexible place. It would hurt too much for the client to answer honestly, so they give the answer that is consistent with their behavior—even though their behavior belies their actual value. Most of the time, the person does not do this consciously. This is just a pattern the person has been in and they have a hard time noticing and stopping it.

If you see this occurring, prolong the discussion on that value. Questions like, "What would you say about this value if nobody would hear your answer?" or "What would you choose if nobody ever saw you do this?" Another way to get in-formation about the reasons behind that choice is to ask, "What scares you about doing something different in this area?" If you have a good relationship with the client, you can even say, "I'm not sure about what you just said. Part of that does not ring true given everything I know about you." Even "Tell me about that" can get the conversation going. I know challenging a client's values is a bit grandiose, but this is our profession and sometimes we can tell if something is off.

WRAP UP WITH HOMEWORK

For the behavioral commitment this week, try to have your client independently set a goal based on a value they identified this session. As usual, use the *Behavioral Commitment Worksheet* (see Appendix C) as your template. If appropriate, ask your client to select a goal outside their comfort zone that they might not have thought to work on before today. Setting slightly more challenging behavioral commitments will tell you how well your client is able to use the skills they have been building in novel situations. These data will, in turn, help you determine how ready your client is for therapy termination. Given the emphasis on values this session, you might even start out the homework discussion with asking your client to choose the value on which they want to actively work, rather than an ac-tion. Once they have identified a value, ask them to generate actions linked to the value. From there, narrow down the behaviors by asking your client which one would be most meaningful for them to do this week. Make sure your questions are only guiding the decision-making process; you want your client to be able to think through these same steps (i.e., choose value, brainstorm actions consistent with the value, select specific action, do the action) when they are making choices outside therapy.

SESSION SUMMARY

This session focused on values. Through reviewing the homework, you should have been able to identify where your client is still struggling and to work on those processes before moving on to values. If your client seems to have a good grasp on the other processes, you can begin values work by defining and clarifying values. Once you and your client have identified their values, you can segue into evaluating behavioral consistency with values and goal setting. As you are approaching the end of therapy, your client might be setting their own homework at this point, and your job is to ensure that they are set up for sustainable success (e.g., by linking actions to values, monitoring the size of behavioral commitments).

REFERENCES

Lundgren, T., Luoma, J. B., Dahl, J., Strosahl, K. D., & Melin, L. (2012). The Bull's-Eye Values Survey: A psychometric evaluation. *Cognitive and Behavioral Practice, 19*(4), 518–526. doi:10.1016/j.cbpra.2012.01.004

Twohig, M. P. & Crosby, J. M. (2008). Values clarification. In W. T. O'Donohue and J. E. Fisher (Eds.), *Cognitive behavior therapy: Applying empirically supported practice techniques in your practice* (2nd ed.) (pp. 583-588). Hoboken NY: John Wiley & Sons. Also appears in W. T. O'Donohue and J. E. Fisher (Eds.), *General principles and empirically supported techniques of cognitive behavior therapy* (pp. 681–686). Hoboken NY: John Wiley & Sons.

Wilson, K. G., Sandoz, E. K., Kitchens, J., & Roberts, M. (2010). The Valued Living Questionnaire: Defining and measuring valued action within a behavioral framework. *The Psychological Record, 60*, 249–272. doi:10.1007/BF03395706

10

Session 10

Values and Behavioral Commitments

We have hopefully built up the acceptance and mindfulness processes by now and are shifting to helping the client use those skills to engage in meaningful activities. We want therapy set up in a way that these skills continue after sessions are over. In this session, we review homework and the values discussion from the last week, and we help the client where we can. Then, we will build on values work and clarify behavioral commitments with the client.

REVIEW HOMEWORK

As in every session, you should review the homework from last week, focusing on behavioral changes the client worked on and how well they practiced psychological flexibility while enacting those changes. In this session, pay particular attention to the client's connection to their values and whether their actions were more influenced by what they care about in life or by their emotional experience. The client was likely able to stay in touch with their values for part of the exercise but then lost that connection later on. Here is how this conversation might go:

THERAPIST (T): Last week we discussed engaging in actions tied to things you care about. Sometimes this is easy—like when your excitement and motivation are high. There are other times when you don't feel so motivated to do it. We talked about how connecting with values can help people find meaning in their actions. Nevertheless, even when there is meaning to the action, you can experience a variety of emotions—which can make the action more difficult. I would like to hear about what you worked on last week. How were you connected with your values, and how did you handle any difficult experiences that showed up during the activity?

CLIENT (C): We agreed I would show courage and stand up for myself at
work three times. We talked about how actual events could look different because I feel small or put down in different situations each
week, although issues with one coworker are common. I found a couple
opportunities to work on this. First, I was in a meeting and we were
discussing solutions to a problem. I had an idea, a solution. Then my
mind started racing about sounding dumb, about what I was going to
say, and on and on. In this moment, I recognized this was what we were
talking about. I was given the chance to practice living while afraid.

T: Tell me what you did.

C: I offered my idea. It came out fine. I'm not the most amazing speaker but
I did fine, and people seemed to appreciate my idea.

T: What did you do with your fear and anxiety during this event?

C: I think I did a good job handling it. It was like a bully at a playground.
It kept poking at me, but I just let it be and did not engage with it. It was
still annoying and I wished it was not there, but by not engaging with it
too much, I could get through my meeting pretty well.

T: Were you in touch with why you were doing this? Another way of asking
my question is: Were you aware of your values in this moment and did
they affect you in any way?

C: That is a good question. I'm not sure. I knew I wanted to do this differently and was not pleased with how I had been handling these situations
in the past. I was motivated to do this differently, but I think the last time
I really linked my actions with my values was in our discussion during
the session.

T: This leads me to my final question: If you were in a situation like this in
the future, would you want to speak up or stay quiet?

C: There is no question I am glad I spoke up. I am pleased I got my opinion
out there. I also think this will help me in my career. People who offer
useful things seem to get more opportunities at my office. I'm not all
about advancing, but I'd like the option.

T: This point goes back to one of our first sessions. Remember when
I offered two games you could play? The first one was unfair and you
played for emotional comfort. The second was fair and you played for
better quality of life. It sounds like you played the second game. I hope
you can hold on to what it was like to intentionally play for better quality
of life because this information can be useful.

It is worth noting, it could have been possible that this client presented her
idea at the meeting and the group disagreed with her. She might have felt sad and
had thoughts about how she often has bad ideas. Prior to our clients practicing
behavioral commitments, we should warn them that we cannot predict how behavioral commitments will go. Sometimes they go really well, sometimes poorly,
and sometimes they land somewhere in between. But if the action is based on a
value, it is likely worth trying. The fact that it did not go well can just teach us

something about how we might do it next time, or whether that is the way we will choose to pursue the value next time. Maybe the client needs to work on her public speaking skills, idea formulation, or timing of offering ideas. Thus, even if her idea had been shot down, the event was a success because she followed her values and learned something about the situation.

The information you get from a discussion like this tells you how well your client is doing in these areas. Again, use the ACT ADVISOR (Figure 2.2.) to determine which processes need more attention as you gather information from your client. For example, based on this example, we would say the client is doing mediocre in terms of values clarity and doing well in terms of behavioral commitments. Thus, you would want to spend more time covering values this session.

REACTIONS TO VALUES FROM LAST WEEK

As we have done with the other processes, we want to check in on values and see how the client is doing on this process. If we had to simplify what we want clients to work on in values work, it would be these two things: (1) to clarify what is important to them and (2) to get in touch with their values and choose to head toward them rather than toward emotional control in moments when they would usually engage in emotional control. Thus, check in with the client on how present their values are in their day-to-day actions, and whether they are checking in with their values when making decisions. You could ask about values by saying something like this:

> T: Last week, when we went over your values, you talked about things like family, work, religion, and your friends and how these were the key things in your life right now. I got the sense that your day-to-day activities were pretty focused on dealing with your anxiety and you were not spending as much time and energy on these values as you would like. Was this week any different?
>
> c: I am not sure I was thinking about these things differently, but I did more things I care about. Maybe I remembered to stop running from anxiety but forgot to think about what I was moving toward.
>
> T: That leads to a little more "white knuckling."
>
> c: I think you are right. I did it, but it was difficult.
>
> T: You are moving in a good direction. Let's talk about putting all these pieces together.

BEING OPEN TO THINGS YOU HATE, TO GET THINGS YOU WANT

When we think about how cognitions affect our actions, one of the biggest things is that our thoughts can make things we once enjoyed aversive and make things we once found aversive enjoyable or worth approaching. For example, the feelings associated with vigorous exercise would be considered scary in a different context. Feeling out of breath, sore, sick, and tired are sought after if one is training for an event or otherwise trying to build fitness. Most of us have done kind things for friends or loved ones that were objectively unpleasant but we found meaning in those acts because we were helping someone we care about. We want to accomplish something similar in this section of treatment. We want to help the client link the difficult steps involved in therapy to their personal values so that the difficulties experienced in therapy are connected to something meaningful. We want to change the context in which inner and outer experiences occur such that even though certain actions continue to be objectively difficult, they also become seen as meaningful. The following example illustrates how this might be described.

> T: Tell me about one of the worst places you have ever been. I don't mean for you to tell me about one of the worst times of your life, but what is one of the most miserable situations you have ever been in? I'm not really looking for a trauma or something like that. I'm looking for something that was more of a chore. I have two that come to mind I want to share as examples. The first was when my wife and I decided we would do a backpacking trip through this lovely part of Wisconsin where we used to live. The trip got delayed because of rain, but after the rain stopped, we headed out. Wisconsin has mosquitoes and we were used to that, but something about that rain and that trail brought them out in clouds. We had been dropped off and pretty much had to get to the next spot by ourselves, so we had to walk all day through clouds of mosquitoes. That was rough. The other one was when my wife and I took a long flight to Sweden—it was really long with all the connections. We get to Sweden at like 7:00 A.M. and could not check in until 3:00 P.M. We were exhausted and had to wander the town without a shower for 8 hours until we could check in. That was rough, too. Tell me about one of your memories like that.
>
> C: I had one where I was trapped in an airport because of weather and poor plane scheduling for like 48 hours. I had on the same clothes, slept on the floor for two nights, had to deal with screaming children. . . . It was terrible.
>
> T: Great. That is the kind of suffering I am looking for. What would you say if I asked you whether you would go through that event again?
>
> C: No way!
>
> T: Right. There is no value in it. We need a reason. Name something in life that is very important to you.
>
> C: My kids.
>
> T: If I could promise that your kids would be healthy, at least through college, but you had to live that event again, would you do it?
>
> C: Of course.

T: Would you do it every year if I offered that your children would be healthy for that year? You'd have to do this every year of your life, but they would have no major health problems as long as you committed to it.

C: Of course.

T: I want you to see a few things here. You immediately said that you would do it. There was no question about it. This is one of the most unpleasant events you have ever gone through, and you were sure you would do it again for your children. This is the power of values. While values are not a cure-all, connecting with values can give meaning to difficult situations. If you need to do something and don't feel like it, see if you can find something about the task that is consistent with your values. I find it helpful to find and connect with different motivating aspects of an activity. For example, if I'm doing homework with my kids and they are whining, I can connect with giving my wife a break from this job or connect with helping my kids live a slightly better life because they understand this material. Usually, connecting with the purpose of an activity makes it easier for me to practice willingness with my frustrations in the moment.

DISCUSSION OF BEHAVIORAL COMMITMENTS

Behavioral commitments are the "final" process of change in ACT, although, technically, your client has already been practicing them through homework assignments since the second session. Behavioral commitments are the one area where you know more about how to implement ACT than we do. This is where you integrate the skills you already know are useful in your specific area. For example, someone who struggles with social interactions would likely benefit from social skills training, whereas someone diagnosed with a substance use disorder would benefit from techniques such as scheduled smoking or fading of use amounts. Exposure exercises are a key part of the treatment of anxiety disorders, and they can be done in an ACT-consistent manner. Lots of people with regimented medical issues can benefit from learning psychological flexibility in addition to the steps for managing their medical issue.

Working from an ACT approach means your client should connect with their values and practice other elements of psychological flexibility while engaging in behavior change. The combination of these two skills is key to making meaningful and lasting change. Other aspects to note when discussing behavioral commitments include the following: (1) any size step is great as long as it is a step in a valued direction, (2) not to base the activity on distress or emotional level, and (3) be present while engaging in the activity (these specific points were covered in Chapter 5). In the following sections, we will go over key points we like to cover with clients, using text addressed to clients.

Think of it like a graph (slowly going up or down)

I'd like to spend a little time talking about following your values and acting on your behavior change plans. One thing that happens when people look at their end goal or where they want to be is that it feels overwhelming. It's like showing up at college and thinking about graduating. There are so many steps you need to take care of and it feels like there isn't time for large road bumps. Graduating from college can seem overwhelming when we think of it as one big step. It is fine that it feels overwhelming; your brain is just doing what it does. It's predicting the future and going through all the issues that can occur. We just need to find a better way to handle this struggle.

I like to think about what we are doing here as a graph like one you'd see for stocks or a business. All we want is for the graph to be going in the right direction. If we are working on more engagement with family, then I am not particularly concerned with where we start. I just hope we can keep increasing things week by week. If we are working on stopping smoking cigarettes, then I hope that number goes down a little bit week by week. If we can keep making little changes, we will eventually get there. Don't forget, we spent a really long time building up this pattern; we are welcome to spend a long time going the other way.

One last thing: Other groups don't get this slow change as much as those of us in mental health do. We see slow change with every client we work with because we are teaching a set of new skills. Learning new things takes time and practice. I would never ask you to learn algebra, another language, or to dance, quickly. These things take practice and feedback, and more practice and more feedback. Learning how to live differently is the same. This is going to take time. So, when outside groups such as your church, family, friends, and coworkers don't understand this, don't blame them. They might think of this like a class where you get the information and now you know it. They might not get that this is learning a whole new set of skills that you get to use in a thousand situations.

Small steps

As I just said, shoot for getting better instead of getting there. There are many things in life that have no shortcut. Changing how you live is a slow process. Focus on whether this week was better than last week, or whether this month was better than last month. Sorry to use a dog as an example, but we just adopted a 3-year-old Chihuahua. She had some skills but was lacking a ton of them. The most annoying behavior was that she went after our cat every time the cat was around; she was totally out of control. I worked at it every day by rewarding behaviors I wanted to see from the dog, and a little for the cat if she stayed in the room. That whole first week was a mess. The second week had some good moments but many rough ones. The third week started to have more good moments than bad, and so on. If you asked me on any one day, I might have been pretty negative about her progress. But if we graphed it, we would have seen the average day improving. If you keep working at it and taking steps in your direction, you will slowly make changes. I don't know when you will get there. Focus on the journey—and someday you will be at a place you are proud of—even if it can be hard to know when and where that place will be.

Steps are toward values rather than away from emotions

This is one of the largest takeaways from ACT. There are a few general rules one can implement on a daily basis that work out positively, and this is one of them. Here it is: *Make actions about pursuing values rather than regulating emotion.* As with all rules, this rule will not be helpful at times, but, in general, our clients would benefit from focusing their actions on pursuing values instead of on regulating emotions. If a client is ever unsure about what to do in life, they can go back to this rule.

If there was one part I hope you take away from our conversation on values and behavior change, it would be to make your actions about pursuing your values rather than moving away from unwanted inner experiences. If we could somehow shift all action that was for emotional control to something that you cared about, think about how much you could get accomplished and how different your life would be. It is a simple shift.

Make this a way of life

My final suggestion is to find a way to keep this going after our sessions. One of the powerful things about therapy is that you have to check in with someone every week. This work stays on your mind every day because someone is going to ask you about it. I hope you can keep the pedal down a little bit. Each person needs to find their own way of doing it. We will talk about this more next week, but make maintaining your mental health a part of your life. If you are not moving in the direction you want to be moving in, think about what you need to be working on. You might be buying into thoughts, running from emotion, or not being present with important things. Spend time on those issues and make small plans for how you are going to keep moving in a valued direction.

WRAP UP WITH HOMEWORK

Just like every other week, have your client make plans for behavior change using the *Behavioral Commitment Worksheet* (see Appendix C). By this time, your client should be proficient at identifying a values-consistent behavioral commitment and a specific process of change that they think would be helpful to work on. Given that you are coming to the end of therapy, we recommend letting your client take the lead here. Giving your client space to think through an appropriate behavioral commitment is also a chance for you to conduct a quick assessment of whether they are prepared to sustain behavior change going forward. For example, if they readily identify a goal and skill that follow from what you two have discussed in recent sessions, this reflects self-awareness and ability to set goals independent from your guidance. However, if your client struggles to select a goal or identifies one that is about emotion regulation, you will need to revisit previous material.

Notes for final session

If you get the sense that your client is ready for treatment termination, ask them to think through a couple points over the next week: (1) How am I going to keep up behavior change? (2) What do I still need to work on? Their answers to these questions will provide useful data for determining how likely they will be able to maintain therapeutic gains.

SESSION SUMMARY

The focus of this session is to explicitly link continued behavioral commitments and values. We hope the client can continue to make notable behavioral commitments tied to values, and that these behavioral commitments move the client in important directions. If this work can keep going, we predict the client will make notable strides in life. In the next session, you will work to encourage the client to keep up with their successes after therapy termination.

11

Session 11

Maintaining Growth

REVIEW HOMEWORK

As this is the last session, the homework review process should be driven more by your client. That is, they should be bringing up areas in which they were successful or struggled with minimal therapist prompting. Their ability to identify these areas will help them troubleshoot and sustain behavioral changes going forward. The homework from the previous session was designed to focus more on behavioral commitments so that your client could start to build up new, more values-consistent patterns of action. See if your client has done so. Ask questions that will guide them to think about how they will work on behavioral commitments without having a therapist with whom to check in weekly. Examples of such questions include the following:

- What will you do with that challenge the next time it shows up?
- How will you keep up your progress?
- What was it like to take this step toward your values? How will you keep taking steps in this direction?
- What if anxiety gets really high? What will you do then?
- What if your mind tells you "you're not good enough" or "you don't deserve a better life"?

These questions are also a way for you to assess where your client is on the ACT ADVISOR (Figure 2.2) or the six ACT processes of change. You will need this information to shape your last session, helping your client build on their strengths and brainstorming ways they can improve skills deficits. Note that termination is not about being 100% psychologically flexible; we believe termination is indicated when your client is prepared to continue practicing psychological flexibility independently. After all, even the most seasoned ACT therapists have their rigid moments.

ASK WHAT HAS BEEN THE MOST USEFUL PART
OF THERAPY

This is consistent with what we have been talking about throughout this book. If people could actually pay attention to the contingencies occurring around them and respond in ways that take advantage of those contingencies, they would likely be functioning pretty well. Thus, it can be useful to have the client look back at the contingencies and see what responses have produced the most useful results. You may ask your client a few of the following questions and see what they say.

- As we wrap up, I find it useful to think about the new things you have tried. I would like to know what you found useful or not useful.
- What change have you made that has had the biggest impact on your life?
- What thing have you stopped doing that has improved things for you most?
- What surprised you most in our work together?
- What are you definitely going to keep doing as time moves forward?

ASK WHERE THE CLIENT PREDICTS THEY WILL
GET STUCK

Based on your client's answers to the previous questions and your conceptualization of them over your time together, talk with them about how they are going to deal with instances of psychological inflexibility that will come up for them in the future. The client likely knows where they have generally experienced improvements and areas where they continue to struggle. Help the client see that these situations will come up and that they are not negative; they are part of facilitating behavior change. Give the client some guidance on additional resources they can use to handle their struggles, such as a mobile app or a book. These resources can help clients continue to practice psychological flexibility and apply it to new challenges after therapy has ended. For example, a client who struggles with family issues and who is attending a wedding in a few months might want to read a self-help book leading into the wedding and focus on triggers that will be at the wedding. If things get harder for a student when the semester starts up, then make plans for how the client will focus on maintaining psychological flexibility when the time comes.

REMINDER ABOUT MOVING IN THE RIGHT DIRECTION

Now is a great time to remind the client about something we discussed at the beginning of treatment: Reduction in internal experience is not the objective;

moving in valued directions is. It can be easy to forget that outside of sessions. The communities in which we live generally focus on how we are feeling. As discussed at other points in the book, how we are doing internally is important and interesting, but it makes for a poor indicator of treatment progress. It is sort of akin to what we are finding about health and weight. Yes, lower weight is generally associated with better health, but increasingly we are finding that what we *do* is much more important, and much more controllable, than how much we weigh. One can eat healthy and exercise a lot but have a high body mass index (BMI). Similarly, someone could have a low BMI but be sedentary, eat poorly, and have poor health. Thus, a better indicator of health is probably what we do (e.g., diet, activity, no smoking), rather than numbers on a scale, which may or may not change. The same goes for internal experiences and overt actions: We can behave how we choose, and what happens internally may not mean a lot.

Remind the client that we are thinking similarly about their mental health. We are focusing on how one is living on a day-to-day basis over any particular level of internal experience. For example, someone who experiences depression might find that no matter how they live their life, they experience some depression. It is likely lower when they are living a values-consistent life, but it may still be present. It might be similar if a loved one is struggling with a significant stressor: They may have distress over it, but the distress does not have to negatively affect the person or interfere with their actions. We would argue it is more important to focus one's energy on responding effectively to the distress than to try to eliminate the distress. Thus, you might say something like this to your client:

THERAPIST (T): Tell me about how things have shifted for you in terms of your treatment goals. In particular, I am curious about how you see having less anxiety versus living an enjoyable life.

CLIENT (C): I used to be really focused on experiencing less anxiety. Actually, it was the only goal I could think of. Through our weeks together, I have come to experience that my anxiety and what I do on a given day are somewhat related but not totally related. I used to think anxiety caused the action, but I am feeling more and more that the relationship between anxiety and what I do is loose.

T: Tell me more.

C: I used to plan my days around how I felt. And then, I usually felt depressed on top of anxious because I was not being active. Now, I choose what I want to do each day and let my emotions come along with me. My anxiety is still present, but some days it is a little lower. My experience of depression is certainly less. One odd thing I have found is I am putting myself in anxiety-provoking situations more frequently, so that has been interesting in terms of how much anxiety I feel. It is almost as though the more fun stuff in life is also more anxiety-provoking.

T: OK. So what do you think this tells us about how you should look at how you are doing over the next year?

C: What do you mean?

T: Should you be paying attention to your anxiety or how you are living day-to-day?

C: How I am living.

T: OK. What is going to get in your way of doing that?

C: Oh, just falling into old routines.

T: Yes, you'll have to keep an eye on that. We'll talk about this more later, but a simple reminder, like keeping this appointment time in your calendar, can be a nice way to tell yourself to check in and see how you are doing with your anxiety and valued living.

ASK CLIENT TO SET WEEKLY REMINDERS IN CALENDAR

We strongly believe in the "power of the appointment." Just having someone to check in with every week can keep us on track. We often tell clients to keep the weekly appointment in their calendars. We suggest the client pause for a moment when the appointment is normally scheduled and ask themselves, "How did I do this last week?" It is worth thinking about, whether they are on a positive trajectory or a negative one.

PROVIDING RESOURCES POST-THERAPY

There are a number of non-therapist options (e.g., books, mobile apps, websites) to keep the practice of psychological flexibility going. You can find a list of resources formatted as a handout you can give your clients in Appendix H, at the end of the book.

TELL CLIENT "MY DOOR IS OPEN"

It has always surprised me how much self-stigma people feel with respect to therapy. We understand attending therapy is difficult. It certainly can make someone feel as though they have made mistakes or are "broken" and are therefore in need of therapy. Hopefully, this fusion with self-stories has lessened and the client can see that they are not their self-evaluations. Thus, their resistance to coming into therapy might be weaker.

The second issue is that the client might have a sense that they have already worked on this particular issue and therefore should not need any more assistance with it. But we know that is not how anxiety, depression, and other difficult inner experiences work. We can get better at responding to them, and we can still have times when we are poor at responding to them. During those times, it can be helpful to get some guidance on how to deal with what one is experiencing.

It would be nice if our clients could see us similarly to how they see other health professionals, such as a dentist, general practitioner, or ophthalmologist. We are not saying there should be annual psychotherapy checkups, but for most of us, there is no stigma associated with going for a dental cleaning, a physical exam, or an eye exam. Yet, we have noticed that many of our clients feel stigma about their first visit to a mental health professional and even the visits after that. Thus, it is worth talking about your willingness to work with the client again in the future should it be needed. You might say something like this:

T: I just want you to know you are very welcome to come back in for booster sessions if you feel you are falling into old patterns. Sometimes, people are responding to their internal events really well and doing a nice job of following their values and for some reason they slip up. Somehow, they get off-track. Rather than continuing down that road of "I lost it; it didn't stick," just come back in for a few more sessions. We can work on getting you back on track.

C: Thanks for saying that. I hope I don't fail at this, though. I'm feeling pretty good right now.

T: Yes, and I want to emphasize coming back in here is not a sign of failure. Take exercising and eating healthy, for example. If someone fell off the wagon in those areas, we wouldn't say they lost it and failed. We'd say they need to get back on track. They might get a personal trainer, pair up with a friend for workouts, use an app, or just generally recommit. Do you think you can look at how you are handling your anxiety the same way?

C: Yes. I mean, I had not really thought about it too much, but I never expected to come back in here. I sort of saw this as a thing that I came here and fixed.

T: OK, then it is good we are discussing this. My guess is you will continue to have ups and downs in your life. Maybe you will be ready for the downs and maybe you won't. If you find yourself in a situation where you are struggling to respond or find you are not handling things the way you want, just contact me and we can get you back on track. Usually, somewhere between two and four sessions is what is needed to do this. Think of me like your doctor, dentist, or ophthalmologist. They help you in their specific areas. I want to be the person who helps you in the mental health area.

C: Cool. Sounds good.

SAY GOODBYE AND THANK CLIENT

I (M.P.T.) am going to credit Jason Luoma for teaching me this next piece. We have emphasized modeling throughout all other aspects of therapy. Now that we are at the very last few pages, let's keep that up. Ending therapy can be a unique and sometimes uncomfortable experience. You just had a fairly close relationship with another person. You probably learned a lot about them. They likely told you

---

things they have told very few—if any—other people, and now you have to say goodbye. And it might be for forever. It is unusual in our lives to build such a close relationship with someone and then say, "This will likely be the last time we see each other." Be honest that you may never see your client again.

Ending therapy is not complicated, but it can be emotionally difficult. As this book is *ACT in Steps*, we suggest wrapping up with these few steps: (1) be honest that ending therapy is weird, (2) thank the client for what you can sincerely thank them for, (3) give them the space to say any parting words they need to say, and (4) say goodbye. These are just suggestions, because how you end therapy is a multifaceted issue and depends on your work setting, population, preferences, and so on. The important part is to remain consistent with an ACT approach, ending this relationship in a way that models and instills openness and meaning to the work being done.

Step 1: Be honest that ending therapy can be uncomfortable

We suggest saying something like this:

> Ending therapy is always odd no matter how many times I do it. I feel like we've become close and certainly come to know each other quite well. We have talked about things you probably don't talk about with many people. And now we will wrap up our relationship. It is possible—or even likely—we won't see each other again. Not many relationships are this way. And we can roll with this. We don't need to pretend we will catch up again. I hope you have benefitted from our work together. I will be here if you would ever like to have booster sessions, but if not, that is totally fine.

Step 2: Thank them for what you can sincerely thank them for

Be genuine. It can be tempting to say overly positive things about your client because you are parting ways, but do not be insincere. If you were not inspired by your client's courage, do not say that. Yet, we do recommend taking a few moments before your last session with a client to pause and consider how this work has been meaningful and what you have appreciated or learned in working with this client. Here is a version of what we usually say:

> I learn something from everyone I work with. The things I learned from you and watching the way you worked through your fears will help me with the next client who is in a similar position. I appreciated how hard you worked in therapy and the ways you kept going even when it was not easy. Therapy is difficult and you did a great job at it. I just want to thank you for allowing me

to work with you. I know you hired me, but it was a worthwhile experience for me, too. We are coming up on time (or have finished the work for this session) and I want to give you the chance to say anything you want to say to me before we wrap up.

Step 3: Give them the space to say any parting words they need to say

This is how a relationship should end: with the space to express how each party has perceived the relationship. This is how real relationships work, and it is good for you to model that to the client. It would be easier to just say "goodbye," but you might as well do it the right way.

Step 4: Say goodbye

If you are a new therapist, there are things you will want to work through, such as what to do if a client brings a gift, wants to hug you goodbye, and so on. Our only suggestion is to model psychological flexibility as you navigate these things. If a client brings you a gift and you think it would be unethical to take it, be honest with the client and talk about how you feel. That modeling will go a long way for that client. The last step generally is to say goodbye, as an acknowledgment that your work together is finished, at least for the time being.

SESSION SUMMARY

In this last session you focused on how to help your client maintain the changes they have made, identifying what has worked well and a plan for future areas where they may get stuck. You likely gave them additional resources, helped them set reminders, and left the door open for future work. Finally, you brought the ACT processes to bear in saying goodbye to your client and ending your course of work with them.

General ACT Principles

1. Be experiential. That is, talk about your client's real-life struggles and the thoughts and feelings that come along with those struggles. Try to bring difficult inner experiences that occur outside of session into the therapy room.
2. Create a psychologically flexible context for your client. Teach, model, and act like it is OK to have all sorts of inner experiences.
   - Disclosures can be a useful means of modeling psychological flexibility.
   - Talk about inner experiences in an ACT-consistent way (e.g., transient, inherently powerless over actions, neither good nor bad).
3. Trust that your client's direct experiences with their environment guide them in an effective direction. Your job is to have them contact these contingencies without verbal interference.
4. Use examples and metaphors relevant to your client. Resist the urge to overexplain metaphors.

Session-by-Session ACT Cheat Sheet

Note: This cheat sheet is more helpful if you have already read the chapters in the book. These session guides are more like cues on a slideshow to help you remember key points to cover in sessions. They do not include details on what each point means.

Session 1
1. Establish treatment goals.
2. Provide orientation to therapy and ACT.
3. Illustrate creative hopelessness. *Metaphor: Two games*
4. Assign homework: Practice willingness.

Session 2
1. Review homework.
2. Address control as the problem.
    a. Workability of emotional/cognitive control. *Exercises: Don't feel anxiety, don't think of . . ., create an emotion, control overt behavior*
    b. Workability of behavioral control.
3. Validate need or desire for control.
4. Introduce acceptance as an alternative.
5. Frame weekly homework as behavioral commitments.
6. Assign homework using *Behavioral Commitment Worksheet* (Appendix C). See the end of this appendix for notes on homework setting and review.

Sessions 3 and 4
1. Review homework.
2. Review acceptance. *Analogy: School teacher*
3. Discuss automaticity of thoughts and fusion.
4. Introduce defusion. *Exercises: Describing versus evaluating experiences, labeling-thoughts mindfulness exercise, breaking the rules*
5. Assign homework using *Behavioral Commitment Worksheet* (Appendix C).

Sessions 5 and 6

1. Review homework.
2. Introduce values to enhance motivation.
3. Review acceptance. *Exercises: Self-compassion, flexible attention with a painful emotion, changing "but" into "and"*
4. Review defusion. *Exercises: Seeing thoughts more concretely*
5. Introduce mindfulness. *Exercise: Putting thoughts on movie screen*
6. Assign homework using *Behavioral Commitment Worksheet* (Appendix C).

Sessions 7 and 8

1. Start with mindfulness exercise. *Exercises: Notice the breath, notice bodily sensations, notice sounds in the room, notice thoughts, notice feelings or urges, take perspective on the past, take perspective on the future, notice observing perspective, notice intentions (values).*
2. Review homework.
3. Review acceptance and defusion as needed. *Exercises: Annoying younger sibling, NOTE acronym* (handout in Appendix E).
4. Introduce self-as-context. *Exercises: You as a home*
5. Assign homework using the *Behavioral Commitment Worksheet* (Appendix C).

Session 9

1. Review homework.
2. Define and clarify values. Use *Valued Living Questionnaire* (VLQ; Appendix F) or *Bull's-Eye Values Survey* (Appendix G).
3. Assess consistency between actions and values.
4. Brainstorm goals based on values.
5. Assign homework using the *Behavioral Commitment Worksheet* (Appendix C).

Session 10

1. Review homework.
2. Review values.
3. Define behavioral commitments and emphasize sustainability of actions. *Analogy: Graph with overall increasing trend*
4. Assign homework using *Behavioral Commitment Worksheet* (Appendix C).

Session 11

1. Review homework.
2. Ask about useful aspects of therapy.
3. Ask about areas that client will struggle with going forward.
4. Encourage moving in a valued direction and brainstorm ways to stay on track.
5. Provide resources (see *Self-Guided ACT Resources* in Appendix H). Include yourself as an option.
6. Say goodbye.

HOMEWORK DISCUSSION

When *setting homework* (i.e., behavioral commitments), choose behaviors that are:

1. Concrete (such that an observer could tell whether it occurred).
2. 90% doable given your client's skill level.
3. Sufficiently challenging to your client.
4. Linked to values.
5. About practicing a specific process of change.

When *reviewing homework*, cover the following points:
1. Did your client complete the homework?
2. What was your client's experience of engaging in valued action (during and after)?
3. What were challenges or barriers they faced?
4. What did they do with or how did they respond to those challenges?

What I am committing to *do* this week:

- Be specific by writing out exactly *what* you will do, *when*, and for *how long*, so that if someone watched you, they would know if you met this commitment or not.
- Remember this is about building patterns one small step at a time. Pick a small goal that you can realistically achieve.

This commitment is important to me because:

While I work on my commitment I will practice:

Practical, external barriers that might get in the way and how I will address them:

- Consider barriers external to you that might make it hard to meet this commitment (time, money, opportunity, what others do). How can you address/prepare for these ahead of time?
- If external factors prevent you from being able to work on your commitment, what could you do instead that would have a similar meaning and importance to you?

I will do the following ahead of time to help meet my commitment:

- Consider reminders you can set (on your phone, sticky notes, etc...)
- Consider ways to make it easier to achieve or get support for your commitment (have what you need set up ahead of time, let supportive friends/family know what you are committing to, etc...)

- **Headspace** (subscription on iOS/Android; https://www.headspace.com/). This is the most widely used commercial mindfulness mobile app available. It includes a wide range of tools to learn about and practice mindfulness.
- **Liberate Meditation** (free on iOS/Android; https://liberatemeditation.com). This app is designed for ethnic minority individuals and includes Dharma talks (25–30 minutes) and guided meditations (5–20 minutes) by Buddhist teachers from marginalized ethnic groups.
- **Mindfulness Coach** (free on iOS/Android; https://mobile.va.gov/app/mindfulness-coach). This app was developed by the Veterans Administration (VA) and provides a range of free mindfulness meditations.
- **Stop, Breathe & Think** (subscription on iOS/Android with some free exercises; https://www.stopbreathethink.com/). This app includes a number of free mindfulness exercises, with suggestions on what to practice based on a quick check-in assessment. A more extended set of mindfulness exercises can be purchased with a subscription.

NOTE Handout

N	**Notice what is happening.**
	What thoughts and feelings are showing up? How are you responding to those thoughts and feelings?
O	**Observe your thoughts and feelings for what they are.**
	Take a step back from your thoughts and feelings and simply watch them with curiosity. Make room for them without getting caught up in their content.
T	**Turn toward your values.**
	What would be important for you to do in this very moment? What value would you like to enact in this space? What would move you closer to the life you want for yourself or the person you want to be?
E	**Engage in what matters.**
	Choose to act, based on your values. Recognize you are 100% in control of your behaviors. You get to decide what you do next.

Valued Living Questionnaire (VLQ)

The following are domains of life that are valued by some people. We are concerned with your subjective experience of your quality of life in each of these domains. One aspect of quality of life involves the importance one places on the different domains of living. Rate the importance of each domain (by circling a number) on a scale of 1 to 10; 1 means that domain is not at all important, and 10 means that domain is very important. Not everyone will value all of these domains, or value all domains the same. Rate each domain according to *your own personal sense of importance.*

DURING THE PAST WEEK

Domain	Not at all important									Extremely important
1. Family relations (other than marriage or parenting)	1	2	3	4	5	6	7	8	9	10
2. Marriage/ Couples/Intimate relations	1	2	3	4	5	6	7	8	9	10
3. Parenting	1	2	3	4	5	6	7	8	9	10
4. Friendships/ Social relations	1	2	3	4	5	6	7	8	9	10
5. Employment	1	2	3	4	5	6	7	8	9	10
6. Education/ Training	2	3	4	5	6	7	8	9	10	
7. Recreation	1	2	3	4	5	6	7	8	9	10
8. Spirituality	1	2	3	4	5	6	7	8	9	10
9. Citizenship/ Community life	1	2	3	4	5	6	7	8	9	10
10. Physical well-being	1	2	3	4	5	6	7	8	9	10

In this section, we would like you to give a rating of how *consistent* your actions are with each value. Everyone does better in some domains than others. We are NOT asking about your ideal in each domain. We want to know how you think you have been doing during the past week. Rate each item (by circling a number) on a scale of 1 to 10; 1 means that your actions have been fully inconsistent with your value, and 10 means that your actions have been fully consistent with your value.

Domain	Not at all important									Extremely important
1. Family relations (other than marriage or parenting)	1	2	3	4	5	6	7	8	9	10
2. Marriage/ Couples/Intimate relations	1	2	3	4	5	6	7	8	9	10
3. Parenting	1	2	3	4	5	6	7	8	9	10
4. Friendships/ Social relations	1	2	3	4	5	6	7	8	9	10
5. Employment	1	2	3	4	5	6	7	8	9	10
6. Education/ Training	1	2	3	4	5	6	7	8	9	10
7. Recreation	1	2	3	4	5	6	7	8	9	10
8. Spirituality	1	2	3	4	5	6	7	8	9	10
9. Citizenship/ Community life	1	2	3	4	5	6	7	8	9	10
10. Physical well-being	1	2	3	4	5	6	7	8	9	10

Wilson, K. G., Sandoz, E. K., Kitchens, J., & Roberts, M. (2010). The Valued Living Questionnaire: Defining and measuring valued action within a behavioral framework. *The Psychological Record, 60,* 249–272.

Bull's-Eye Values Survey (BEVS)

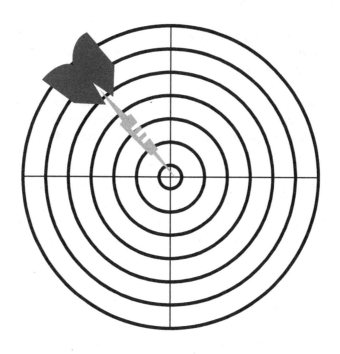

BULLSEYE

The bullseye dartboard is divided into four areas of living that are important in people's lives: work/education, leisure, relationships, and personal growth/ health.

1) *Work/Education* refers to your career aims, your values about improving your education and knowledge, and generally feeling of use to those close to you or to your community (i.e., volunteering, overseeing your household, etc.).

2) *Leisure* refers to how you play in your life and how you enjoy yourself, your hobbies, or other activities that you spend your free time doing (e.g., gardening, sewing, coaching a children's soccer team, fishing, playing sports).

3) *Relationships* refers to intimacy in your life and relationships with your children, your family of origin, your friends, and social contacts in the community.

4) *Personal growth/health* refers to your spiritual life, either in organized religion or personal expressions of spirituality, exercise, nutrition, and addressing health risk factors such as drinking, drug use, smoking, and weight.

In this exercise, you will be asked to look more closely at your personal values in each of these areas and write them out. Then, you will evaluate how close you are to living your life in keeping with your values. You will also take a closer look at the barriers or obstacles in your life that stand between you and the kind of life you want to live. Don't rush through this; just take your time.

PART 1. IDENTIFY YOUR VALUES

Start by describing your *values* within each of the four values areas. Think about each area in terms of your dreams, like you have the possibility to get your wishes completely fulfilled. What are the qualities that you would like to get out of each area, and what are your expectations from these areas of your life? Your value should not be a specific goal but instead reflect a way you would like to live your life over time. For example, getting married might be a goal you have in life, but it just reflects your value of being an affectionate, honest, and loving partner. To accompany your son to a baseball game might be a goal; to be an involved and interested parent might be the value. **Note:** *Write your value for each area on the lines provided next.* It is **your** personal values that are important in this exercise.

Work/education: _____

_____

Leisure: _____

_____

Relationships: _____

_____

Personal growth/health: _____

_____

Now, look again at the values you have written above. Think of your value as "bullseye" (the middle of the dart board). Bullseye is exactly how you want your life to be—a direct hit, where you are living your life in a way that is consistent with your value. Now, make an X on the dart board in each area that best represents where you stand today. An X in the bullseye means that you are living completely in keeping with your value for that area of living. An X far away from the bullseye means that your life is way off the mark in terms of how you are living your life.

Since there are four areas of valued living, you should mark **four X's** on the dart board. **Note:** *Use the dart board on this page before you go to Part 2 of this exercise.*

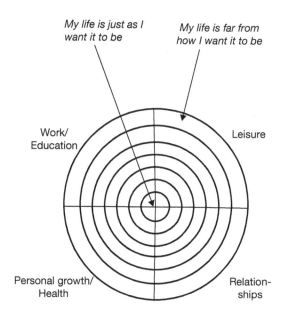

PART 2: IDENTIFY YOUR OBSTACLES

Now write down what stands between you and living your current life as you want to and what you have written in your areas of value. When you think of the life you want to live and the values that you would like to put in play, what gets in the way of you living that kind of life? Describe any obstacle(s) on the lines that follow.

_____

_____

_____

_____

Now estimate to what extent the obstacle(s) you just described can prevent you from living your life in a way that is in keeping with your values. Circle one number that best describes how powerful this obstacle(s) is in your life.

$$1 \quad\quad 2 \quad\quad 3 \quad\quad 4 \quad\quad 5 \quad\quad 6 \quad\quad 7$$

Doesn't prevent me at all   Prevents me completely

PART 3. MY VALUED ACTION PLAN

Think about actions you can take in your daily life that would tell you that you are zeroing in on the bullseye in each important area of your life. These actions could be small steps toward a particular goal, or they could just be actions that reflect what you want to be about as a person. Usually, taking a valued step includes being willing to encounter the obstacle(s) you identified earlier and to take the action anyway. *Try to identify at least one value-based action you are willing to take, in each of the four areas listed here.*

Work/education: _____

_____

Leisure: _____

_____

Relationships: _____

_____

Personal growth/health: _____

_____

Self-Guided ACT Resources

The following is a collection of self-guided resources you can use to continue to learn about and apply ACT in your life. We included books, mobile apps, and online resources that are designed for people like yourself who are looking to apply ACT in their lives.

ACT BOOKS

The following are a set of ACT books we especially recommend for targeted areas. These books typically start from the beginning by walking you through the ACT approach, which we find can be a useful review and reminder for what you have learned in therapy. There are many ways to practice ACT, so this will also help you find new ways to apply ACT in your life.

- **Depression:** Strosahl, K. D., & Robinson, P. J. (2017). *The Mindfulness and Acceptance Workbook for Depression: Using Acceptance and Commitment Therapy to Move Through Depression and Create a Life Worth Living*. Oakland, CA: New Harbinger Publications.
- **Anxiety:** Forsyth, J. P., & Eifert, G. H. (2016). *The Mindfulness and Acceptance Workbook for Anxiety: A Guide to Breaking Free from Anxiety, Phobias, and Worry Using Acceptance and Commitment Therapy*. Oakland, CA: New Harbinger Publications.
- **Social anxiety:** Fleming, J. E., & Kocovski, N. L. (2013). *The Mindfulness and Acceptance Workbook for Social Anxiety and Shyness: Using Acceptance and Commitment Therapy to Free Yourself from Fear and Reclaim Your Life*. Oakland, CA: New Harbinger Publications.
- **Trauma:** Follette, V., & Pistorello, J. (2007). *Finding Life beyond Trauma: Using Acceptance and Commitment Therapy to Heal from Post-Traumatic Stress and Trauma-Related Problems*. Oakland, CA: New Harbinger Publications.

- **Substance use problems**: Wilson, K. G., & DuFrene, T. (2012). *The Wisdom to Know the Difference: An Acceptance and Commitment Therapy Workbook for Overcoming Substance Abuse*. Oakland, CA: New Harbinger Publications.
- **Weight concerns:** Lillis, J., Dahl, J., & Weineland, S. M. (2014). *The Diet Trap: Feed Your Psychological Needs and End the Weight Loss Struggle Using Acceptance and Commitment Therapy*. Oakland, CA: New Harbinger Publications.
- **ACT for teenagers:** Ciarrochi, J. V., Hayes, L. L., & Bailey, A. (2012). *Get Out of Your Mind and Into Your Life for Teens: A Guide to Living an Extraordinary Life*. Oakland, CA: New Harbinger Publications.
- **General ACT book written by the primary developer of ACT, Steven C. Hayes:** Hayes, S. C. (2005). *Get Out of Your Mind and Into Your Life: The New Acceptance and Commitment Therapy*. Oakland, CA: New Harbinger Publications.
- **Mindfulness:** Stahl, B., & Goldstein, E. (2010). *A Mindfulness-Based Stress Reduction Workbook*. Oakland, CA: New Harbinger Publications.

You can also visit https://www.newharbinger.com/psychsolve for help finding a self-help book or https://contextualscience.org/amazon_self_help_bookstore for a full list of ACT books.

ACT MOBILE APPS

Presented here are ACT and related mobile apps that can help you continue to practice what you have learned in therapy through your smartphone. This list was created in 2019, but you can review a continually updated list of mental health mobile apps at PsyberGuide (https://psyberguide.org/).

- **ACT Coach** (free on iOS/Android; https://mobile.va.gov/app/act-coach): This app was developed by the Veterans Administration (VA) and includes a variety of tools to help you practice ACT.
- **ACT Companion** ($3–$15 on iOS/Android; http://www.actcompanion.com/): This app was developed by Russ Harris (a leading ACT trainer) and provides a variety of tools to practice ACT.
- **ACTive: Value-Based Living** (free on iOS only; https://itunes.apple.com/us/app/active-value-based-living/id1343994479): This app provides tools to monitor and set values-based goals.
- **Mindfulness apps:** There are a variety of mindfulness apps available, but here are a couple we especially recommend:
  - **Headspace** (subscription on iOS/Android; https://www.headspace.com/)

- **Stop, Breathe & Think** (subscription on iOS/Android: https://www.stopbreathethink.com/)
- **Mindfulness Coach** (free on iOS/Android; https://mobile.va.gov/app/mindfulness-coach)

ONLINE ACT RESOURCES

The following are a few key ACT websites and online resources we recommend:

- **ACT Guide** (https://scce.usu.edu/services/act-guide/): This is a self-guided course we developed at Utah State University. For a small fee, users can go through the 12-session program, learning key ACT principles and how to apply them in their life.
- **The Happiness Trap Online** (https://thehappinesstrap.com/8-week-program/): This is another self-guided course you can subscribe to that is designed to teach key ACT principles.
- **ACT for the Public Website** (https://contextualscience.org/act_for_the_public): This website is maintained by the Association for Contextual Behavioral Science, the professional home of ACT. It includes a variety of resources for people like yourself looking to apply ACT in their lives.
- **ACT for the Public Listserv** (https://contextualscience.org/emailing_lists#ACTPUBLIC): This is a long-standing email listserv in which people share about their experiences applying ACT in their lives and get help from others doing the same.
- **ACT Facebook Group** (https://www.facebook.com/groups/ACTsupport/): This is a Facebook group designed for people to support each other in applying ACT in their lives.

Michael P. Twohig, PhD, is a licensed psychologist in the state of Utah and a Professor of Psychology at Utah State University. He received his BA and MS from the University of Wisconsin-Milwaukee, his PhD from the University of Nevada, Reno, and completed his clinical internship at the University of British Columbia Hospital. He is past-President of the Association of Contextual Behavioral Science, the organization most associated with Acceptance and Commitment Therapy (ACT). His research focuses on the use of ACT across a variety of clinical presentations with an emphasis on obsessive compulsive and related disorders. He has published over 100 peer-reviewed articles and three books: *An ACT-Enhanced Behavior Therapy Approach to the Treatment of Trichotillomania* (with Woods), *ACT Verbatim for Depression and Anxiety* (with Hayes), and *Innovations in Acceptance and Commitment Therapy* (with Levin and Krafft). His research has been funded through multiple sources including the National Institute of Mental Health.

Michael E. Levin, PhD, is an Associate Professor of Psychology at Utah State University and a licensed psychologist in the state of Utah. He received his PhD in Clinical Psychology from the University of Nevada, Reno, under the mentorship of Dr. Steven C. Hayes and completed his predoctoral internship at the Brown University Clinical Psychology Training Consortium. Dr. Levin's research focuses on online and self-guided Acceptance and Commitment Therapy (ACT) interventions to improve the reach and impact of mental health services, which has been supported by funding sources including the National Institute of Health. He has published over 100 articles and book chapters, primarily on ACT. Dr. Levin has published two previous books: *Innovations in Acceptance and Commitment Therapy* (with Twohig and Krafft) and *Mindfulness and Acceptance for Addictive Behaviors* (with Hayes).

Clarissa W. Ong, MS, is a fifth-year doctoral student in the Combined Clinical/ Counseling Psychology program at Utah State University. She received her BA from Smith College. Her research interests include developing and testing process-based interventions for anxiety and obsessive-compulsive-related concerns and psychometric evaluation of clinical measures.

Figures and tables are indicated by *f* and *t* following the page number.